After His Likeness

VOLUME VIII in the TRUETT MEMORIAL SERIES

AFTER HIS LIKENESS

by

GEORGE W. TRUETT, D.D., L.L.D.

Compiled and Edited by
Powhatan W. James, Th.D., D.D.

WM. B. EERDMANS PUBLISHING COMPANY
Grand Rapids   1954   Michigan

PRINTED IN THE UNITED STATES OF AMERICA

DEDICATION

This and other volumes
of sermons and addresses
in this series by Dr. George W. Truett
are dedicated to
his beloved
First Baptist Church, Dallas, Texas
where most of them
were delivered

FOREWORD

The late Dr. Douglas Southall Freeman, Virginia's foremost citizen, editor, biographer and historian, in 1939 said of Dr. George W. Truett: "He is one of the most notable figures of twentieth-century Christianity—a man to whom, along with millions of Americans, I owe a debt in spirit." There were many reasons for Dr. Freeman's estimate, one of them being the fact that Dr. Truett ever proclaimed a very high standard of conduct for Christians and always practiced what he preached.

Every sermon in this volume emphasizes some phase of Christian living, such as witnessing, resisting evil, obedience, dedication of life, stewardship, giving Christ first place. For this reason the title *After His Likeness* is given to this volume.

Three sermons herein were first published in 1915 by Fleming H. Revell Co. of New York in a volume of sermons by Dr. George W. Truett which was compiled and edited by Dr. J. B. Cranfill. The title of that first volume of Dr. Truett's sermons was *We Would See Jesus*. It is now out of print and the Fleming H. Revell Company has graciously given permission to reprint these sermons in re-edited form. Your present compiler and editor greatly appreciates this favor, because these particular sermons seem to fit so well in *After His Likeness* and also because they are so worthy of reprinting. They are: "We Would See Jesus," "The Temptation of Our Saviour," and "The Supreme Gift to Jesus." That first volume of Truett sermons went through seventeen printings, a high tribute to the value of the messages therein.

What was said of Abel may also be said of George W. Truett: "He being dead yet speaketh."

Powhatan W. James

Dallas, Texas
August 1, 1954

C O N T E N T S

CHAPTER I

We Would See Jesus

CHAPTER I

We Would See Jesus

~~~~~~

We would see Jesus.
—John 12:21

THE AGE-LONG CRY of the human race has been for the revelation of a personal God, able and willing to forgive human sin and to give rest to the human conscience. From the days of Job, man's cry has been: "Oh, that I knew where I might find him!" Plato voiced such a cry when he said, "We look for a God-inspired man, who will show us our duty and take away the darkness from our eyes." Through long generations of Jewish history there thrilled the longing, voiced in the prophetic hope of a coming Messiah, able and willing to meet man's deepest needs. In the fullness of time he came, and the fame of his words and deeds soon filled the land. A great feast was had in Jerusalem, and along with the thousands who attended it there came some Greeks, whose request also was: "We would see Jesus." That was the first voice from the outside world that gave a hint of the awakening of its sleeping conscience to the fact that Jesus was to be the Saviour and Sovereign over the Gentile as well as the Jewish world.

Marvelous was the impression made upon Jesus by that request of the Greeks. It came at an hour when his work seemed ready to fail; but from that hour there was a new tone of triumph in his words. No more do we hear his plaintive cry over unbelieving Jerusalem but his thoughts are bravely turned towards Calvary. "The hour is come that the Son of Man should be glorified. Verily, verily, I say unto you, except a grain of wheat fall into the ground and die, it abideth alone; but if it die, it bringeth forth much fruit." He speaks again: "Now is my soul troubled; and what shall I say? Father, save me from this hour: but for this cause came I unto this hour. Father, glorify thy name. Then came there a voice from heaven, saying, 'I have glorified it and will glorify it again.' " His heart thrills with the sense of his glorious mission, and he speaks again: "Now is the judgment of this world; now shall the prince of this world be cast out. And I, if I be lifted up from the earth, will draw all men unto me."

Why should we see Jesus? We may well wish to see him because of what he was and is in his own personality. He was both God and man, the God-man in one person. Never did hyphen elsewhere mean so much as here, the God-man. It both joins and divides. It marks distinction and yet unity. Jesus was as really God as though he were never man, and as really man as though he were never God. In the face of this truth, well might the chief apostle say: "Without controversy, great is the mystery of godliness: God was manifest in the flesh, justified in the Spirit, seen of angels, preached unto the Gentiles, believed on in the world, received up into glory." The most stupendous truth ever submitted to human thought is that stated in John's five simple words: "The Word was made flesh."

In the study of Jesus we need always to begin with his humanity. That is where the early disciples began, and that is the rational order. A proper conception of his humanity must be the basis for a proper understanding of his divine nature and work.

In these days men sometimes tell of their difficulties concerning the deity of Jesus, rather than his humanity. In the earlier days, unbelief made its stoutest assaults upon his humanity. The earlier heresies were gnostic heresies that denied that Jesus was really a man. One school of gnostics held that

14

the body of Jesus did not belong essentially to his nature, but that the Messiah descended upon Jesus at his baptism, and left him before his death. Another school held that his body was but a mere illusion, a veneer of human nature, with God-hood hidden behind the face of a man. And still another school held that his body was a body from heaven, having nothing in common with earth.

Against all such theories the title which Jesus chose for himself attests his true and real humanity. "He took not on him the form of angels; but he took on him the seed of Abraham." He was a vital part of the race that he came to save, bone of its bone and flesh of its flesh. He had a human mother and a human birth. He grew, as did others, in wisdom and in stature. His feelings and needs were as those of other men. He was weary and hungry and thirsty. He craved human companionship and sympathy. He was "a man of sorrows and acquainted with grief." "Wherefore, in all things, it behooved him to be made like unto his brethren, that he might be a merciful and faithful High Priest, in all things pertaining to God to make reconciliation for the sins of the people."

Behold him, not "A Son of Man," but "The Son of Man," for all humanity was summed up in him. He was the one perfect, ideal, complete man. "Which of you convinceth me of sin?" was and is his fearless challenge. "I find no fault in him" was and is the universal testimony of his friends and foes. In himself Jesus combines all those gracious qualities that abode severally in his people. All other men have but fragmentary goodness and greatness; that of Jesus is complete, perfect, wanting nothing. The search-light of criticism has been focused on Jesus through the long centuries, and yet it has failed to find in him one suggestion of sin, one ill-spoken word, one selfish deed. Men talk about not believing in miracles. What will they do with Jesus of Nazareth? He

15

is the preeminent miracle of all the ages. Who was that one and only perfect man? Was he not more than a man?

The only rational solution of the humanity of Jesus is the acknowledgment of his deity. For men to laud Jesus as a great and good man, while they repudiate his deity, is to involve themselves in logical contradictions and moral inconsistencies which it is impossible either to reconcile or understand. Remember the claims that this wise and holy One makes for himself: "I am the light of the world." "No man cometh unto the Father but by me." "He that hath seen me hath seen the Father." "I and the Father are one." "Come unto me, all ye that labor and are heavy laden and I will give you rest." If Jesus Christ be not more than a man, what must be thought of the presumption and vanity of these mighty claims? How is it that man's conscience accepts without protest or hesitancy these mighty claims? That question must forever remain an insoluble mystery on any other premise than that Jesus was God manifest in the flesh, in whom dwells all the fullness of the God-head bodily.

From his cradle to his grave the proofs of his Godhead were, in his own person, finding constant illustration. The shepherds came to salute him as king, and the magi, with their rich gifts, came from the Far East to worship him, while he was yet a tiny babe upon his mother's heart. While a lad only twelve years of age, his superlative wisdom utterly astounded the learned doctors in the Temple. As a young man he patiently wrought at the workman's bench, teaching us how the Infinite One can calmly wait, girt with the consciousness of his divine mission. When he came to prosecute his public ministry he had only to speak the word and the winds were hushed, the storms calmed, the hungry thousands fed, the sick made well and the dead brought back to life. He lived as none other ever lived. He died as none other ever died, and from Olivet he went back to his Father the consummator of history, the victorious Saviour of a lost world.

"We would see Jesus," not only because of what he is in his matchless person, but, also, because of what he is and does for man. He is man's Saviour from sin. "Thou shalt call his name Jesus, for he shall save his people from their sins." If Jesus were merely a perfect example or a matchless teacher for man, then he could not encompass man's deepest needs. Sin is the terrible tragedy, the intolerable yoke in every human life. Our highest and eternal joy in seeing Jesus is in seeing him as our Saviour from sin. By his expiatory death on the cross, "the just for the unjust," Jesus answers the eternally vital question how a guilty sinner may have forgiveness and salvation and happiness here and forevermore.

> Forever God, forever man,
> My Jesus shall endure:
> And fixed on him my hope remains
> Eternally secure.

It was said of Mozart that he brought angels down, and of Beethoven that he lifted mortals up. Jesus does both and more. He is God's way to man, he is man's way to God, the true Jacob's ladder between earth and heaven.

And the glorious truth is that his gospel may be put into the crucible of human experience. Man may personally know whether Jesus can give peace to the troubled conscience, whether he can give light for life's bedarkened problems, whether he can give healing for earth's staggering sorrows. The world is filled with men and women, this hour, who vainly sought everywhere for peace and light and help, but they found them not until they found them in Jesus. These men and women tested him, and in their deepest consciousness they know better than they know anything else that through him their darkness was dispelled, their burdens lifted, their victories won. Tell me how it is that, of all the sons of men since the world began, it was never heard that a man was saved by Plato, or by Socrates, or by any one else but by

17

Jesus Christ alone. How is it that he alone has been able really to redeem men from the fatal grip of appetite and passion and sin? There can be but one logically intelligent answer, and that answer is that in Jesus Christ we have the only begotten Son of God, Who is the Lamb of God, the Light of the World, the one divine and all-sufficient Saviour.

How may we see Jesus? May we see Jesus today? Not, to be sure, with our physical eyes, but with the eyes of the mind and heart. May we approach him, realize him, be conscious of his personal presence and help, even as we are conscious of the presence and help of parent or teacher or dearest earthly friend? These are vital questions that go to the depths of our hearts. I make bold to answer them that Jesus may be, ought to be, more real to us than is any other person in all the world. Jesus is not some mere theory, some inspiring memory, some vague, personal influence; but he is a Person, to be approached, to be felt, to be trusted, to be loved, and to be obeyed even unto death. How may we thus see Jesus as we are daily driven by the manifold problems and duties of the earthly life?

If we would see Jesus, we must make much of his Book. If we would know a person, we must understand him. If we would trust a person, then our trust must be based on knowledge. Jesus cannot be seen, will not be graciously real to the man who neglects the Bible. It is true that "the heavens declare the glory of God, and the firmament showeth his handiwork." But, left to nature, the Bible taken away, man cannot know of God's tenderness and love, cannot know how to love and trust and obey him properly. Though man might name every star that blazes in the eternal depths; though he might map the heavens and tell the constellations as his familiar friends; though he might understand the voice of the flowers; though he might catch the monologues of the mountains, the dirges of the oceans, the symphonies of the spheres; though all nature might speak to him the mighty secrets of its origin and Maker, in all this man would see only the majesty and mightiness of God. In God's hand would be the sword of justice, on his lips the word of wisdom, and around him the resplendent robe of righteousness, at once man's envy and despair. Only in the Bible may man learn of the mercy of God in the forgiveness of sins through Jesus Christ.

God's book must be read, and read humbly, reverently, earnestly, continuously, if we would see much of Jesus. If you have read the life of Chinese Gordon, one of the noblest Christians of his or any other age, you discerned that the secret of that wonderful life was in the fact that he spent long hours every day in the study of the Bible. He had many books in the Soudan, but this was the testimony that he left concerning them: "I may as well part with all my books except two, the Bible and the Concordance, so far as they contain essential knowledge."

b. If we would see Jesus, we must know much of secret prayer—mark you, of secret prayer. Secret prayer is the unerring thermometer to our life of prayer. If ever we are sincere in prayer, it is when we are in secret prayer. It is then, if ever, that we are conscious of God. Jesus said, "But thou, when thou prayest, enter into thy closet, and when thou hast shut thy door, pray to thy Father which is in secret; and thy Father which seeth in secret shall reward thee openly." How much do we give ourselves to secret prayer? Is it not just here that most of all we fail? We go about the doing of many things, but is not secret prayer one of the things that we largely leave undone? It takes time to become spiritual, and time spent alone with God is the best spent time in all one's life.

c. Again, if we would see Jesus, we must watch against sin, with uncompromising warfare. There must be absolute sincerity and whole-hearted thoroughness at this point. That were but hollow mockery for a man to pray for forgiveness,

19

his own heart the while burning with hatred and festering with grudges against some fellow creature. The amputating knife of genuine repentance must be put to sin, if we would hope for the smile of Jesus and for the benefit of his blood which cleanseth from all sin. God cannot afford to answer some men's prayers! For him to do so would be to put a premium upon sin. The hidden wedge of gold and the Babylonish garment must be disclosed and restored if men may hope for answered prayer. It is sin that separates between man and God. Sin is a veil through which Jesus cannot be seen. Sin is an insulator that cuts off the currents between man and God. It is "the supplication of a righteous man that availeth much." "If I regard iniquity in my heart, the Lord will not hear me."

No man who is not keenly sensitive to sin can know much or see much of Jesus. "Blessed are the pure in heart, for they shall see God"—see him here and now in daily experience. "Who shall ascend into the hill of the Lord? Or who shall stand in his holy place? He that hath clean hands and a pure heart, who hath not lifted up his soul unto vanity or sworn deceitfully. He shall receive the blessing of the Lord, and righteousness from the God of his salvation." Oh, what need we have for frequent and most rigid self-examination, that we may become increasingly sensitive to every approach of sin! And we are to watch with all diligence against the little sins. It was the little foxes that spoiled the vines. If we carelessly cherish what may seem to us to be inconsequential sins—for example, pride, which goeth before destruction, and envy, which is as rottenness in the bones —these sins will consume us as doth a cancer and more and more will they hide from us the face of Jesus.

If we would see Jesus, we need to magnify the blessedness of Christian fellowship. In the old-fashioned experience-meeting men and women came together just to tell, timidly though joyfully, what they saw and felt and knew of the things of

Jesus — would to God our churches had it back again! "Then they that feared the Lord spake often one to another, and the Lord harkened and heard it, and a book of remembrance was written before him for them that feared the Lord, and that thought on his name." Sometimes a preacher's sermonic fires burn low, and not a text will give up its treasures, dig for them though he may. What does the preacher do? Let such preacher find and talk with some one who has a vital knowledge of the saving grace of God, and sermonic fires will immediately burn again.

Once again, if we would see Jesus, we must be busy for him. The indolent Christian cannot see much or know much of Jesus. Idleness is one of the most terrible foes to grace. It is the flowing stream that is the healthy stream. The stagnant pond breeds miasma and malaria and death. Many a Christian who is spiritually sick, he knows not why, would thrill with a new joy and new visions of Jesus if only he would be busy for him. Doubt, unbelief, despondency are all dispelled by activity. It is the man who does Christ's will unto whom is revealed his doctrine.

And still again, if we would see Jesus as we ought and as we may, we must give ourselves completely to his guidance and government. Jesus will be lord of all, or he will not be lord at all. The reason so many people get so little out of their religion is that they put so little into it. If men would see Jesus and thus experience the deepest of joys, and from him have the noblest victories in their lives, then, for all this, they must pay the requisite price. Paul paid such price. Gladly did he suffer the loss of all things, home, kindred, inheritance, comforts, country, life itself, that he might have the excellency of the knowledge of Christ Jesus, his Lord. Do you wonder that he had visions and revelations which could not be put into speech? Do you wonder that his letters abound in doxologies, as he contemplates the unfolding glory of his Lord? Paul paid the price for his glorious visions of Jesus.

Carl.

Here, then, is the vital question for us. Will we pay the price to see Jesus as we need to see him, as he would have us see him? Are we willing to live for him, to put him first, to do his will, be what it may, lead where it will? Right here is the supreme battle of the Christian life. It is the battle between Christ and self. The self-centered life will not see Jesus, and must surely fail. The Christ-centered life will mount higher and higher in its visions of Jesus, and will more and more exult in the victory that overcomes the world.

Oh, men and women, if we will pay the price, we may daily see Jesus—may know that he walks with us, talks with us, and lives with us, and lives in us, our certain help for every day and duty of earth. And thus seeing him and serving him, brighter and better shall be all our days, even unto that blissful day when we shall pass through the gates of the celestial city, where we shall be "like him, for we shall see him as he is."

CHAPTER II

A Witness Sent from God

A Witness Sent from God

~~~~~~~~~~~~~~~~~~~~~~~~~~~~

> *There was a man sent from God, whose*
> *name was John. The same came for a*
> *witness, to bear witness of the Light,*
> *that all men through him might believe.*
> —JOHN 1:6-7
>
> *He was a burning and a shining light.*
> —JOHN 5:35

FROM the Gospel of John, the beloved apostle, I have chosen two statements concerning John the Baptist as a basis for our study today. The first is a statement of John in the prologue to his Gospel. The second is a declaration from the lips of Jesus made to the Jewish authorities at Jerusalem about John, the forerunner of Jesus, the same man to whom, on another occasion, Jesus paid the highest possible tribute when he said, "Among them that are born of women there hath not risen a greater than John the Baptist."

It is good to study Bible portraits of great men and women. John the Baptist is one of the most arresting characters presented to us by the Scriptures. At this time I desire to direct your attention to him because in him we note three of the qualifications which must characterize every effective witness for Christ. These are: the credentials of the witness, the intelligent zeal of the witness, and the effective mission of the witness.

John, known as the "Baptizer," was divinely accredited. He was sent from God, and his character and witness were endorsed by Jesus. And Gabriel, the angel of the Lord, announced to Zacharias that John would be great in the sight of the Lord and would be filled with the Holy Spirit, and would turn many of the children of Israel unto the Lord their God. Never was mortal man more fully accredited. Even before his birth he bore the stamp of heaven's approval upon him. And at his birth, his father was filled with the Holy Spirit and prophesied, saying, "And thou, child, shalt be called the prophet of the Most High: for thou shalt go before the face of the Lord to make ready his ways."

It seems to me to be well for us to emphasize the importance of John the Baptist, or any other witness for Christ, having a conviction of being sent as a witness. John had such a conviction and that accounts for the urgency, the boldness, and the authority with which he bore his witness. There can be no doubt of that!

The truth of the matter is that every great and effective witness for God has had a conviction that he or she was sent of God. Even Jesus himself said no less than sixteen times that he was sent on his earthly mission by his heavenly Father.

You have read the Bible carelessly if you have not observed that it constantly stresses the fact that all of God's great servants were motivated and empowered by the consciousness of having a God-given mission. A few examples will illustrate the point. Moses told Pharaoh that God had sent him. and proved it by many works. Because Elijah was conscious of being God's messenger he was emboldened to condemn wicked Ahab, the king, and challenge the false prophets on Mount Carmel. Nathan, the prophet, was sent of God and hesitated not to point the accusing finger at David, the mighty king, and pronounce doom upon his family because of David's great sins in having Uriah slain and taking Bathsheba as one of his wives. The list of heroic witnesses and workers for God could be extended across all the centuries. In every instance we would find an individual mastered by the conviction that he was sent of God.

Not long before Jesus returned to his heavenly glory he was praying to his heavenly Father about his disciples and he said, "As thou didst send me into the world, even so sent I them into the world." And his last words on earth to his disciples, and to us also, were these: "Ye shall receive power when the Holy Spirit is come upon you: and ye shall be my witnesses both in Jerusalem, and in all Judea and Samaria, and unto the uttermost part of the earth." The Christian world is well agreed that those words were intended for Christ's followers today no less than for those disciples who stood with him on the Mount of Olives so long ago.

If, deep down in your heart, you believe that Christ wants you to witness for him in the power of the Holy Spirit, and are willing to have it so, then you can be hopeful, you can be strong, you can be equal to the task, you can have the conviction that you also are a man or a woman sent from God. Every Christian ought often to ask himself the question, "Am I carrying out God's plan for my life?" If the conviction be clear to you that you are, then you can truly say, "I am sent from God." People are sent from God to be preachers, merchants, lawyers, doctors, teachers, farmers, mechanics, musicians, writers, missionaries and all other worthy undertakings. Anyone who holds that spiritual view of his or her vocation can live a victorious life. If you are where God wants you to be, and if you are doing what God wants you to do, then you are divinely sent, even as John the Baptist was sent.

Jesus said that John was "a burning and a shining light." That means that John had both zeal and intelligence, which is a glorious combination in anyone, a combination of heat and light. Zeal needs to be tempered by intelligence and intelligence needs the warmth of a zealous heart. Either, without the other, is lacking in full effectiveness. Sometimes

27

there is heat without any light, and sometimes there is light without any heat. A Christian should be both a burning and shining light. When you see some Christian workers you could heartily wish that they had more sense; and when you see others of them you could heartily wish they had more heat, more heart, more zeal, for they are more like glistening icicles than burning candles.

John gave forth both heat and light. He had the fire and the fire gave out light. His intelligence glowed with fervor. Zeal is both gracious and blessed, but much more so when guided by God-given intelligence.

These observations provide a strong argument for the services rendered by Christian education in our church schools. The Christian college is a divine institution, provided it gives Christ and his gospel their rightful place in classroom, laboratory, library, dormitory and on athletic fields, as well as in the chapel. The denominational college which is thoroughly Christian in tone as well as title has vital values which the secular college does not and cannot have. That is because the values of religion are in many respects superior to the values of the arts and sciences. I do not believe that any denominational college should promote hurtful and obnoxious sectarianism. It is unchristian to the extent that it does. But I do believe that every denominational college, be it Protestant, Catholic, Baptist, or what have you, should faithfully, continually and unhesitatingly emphasize, exemplify, teach and practice the principles and spirit of New Testament Christianity.

All the religious groups called denominations need a constant supply of intelligent, warm-hearted, and well-trained leaders, such as preachers, teachers, officers, musicians, editors, missionaries. The secular schools provide very few of these leaders. The vast majority of those who are burning and shining lights, and therefore leaders, are furnished by the church colleges. I shall ever be thankful that the professors who taught me when I was in college were prayer-meeting Christians, every one of them. God be praised when our Christian colleges magnify and glorify true religion as the most important thing in life, for then they will turn out young men and women of sterling Christian character such as the world so sorely needs. Yes, this world needs burning and shining lights in every realm, in every vocation, in every community. We should pray that God will send among us multitudes of his accredited witnesses who shall be burning and shining lights like this man sent from God, whose name was John.

The third thing we note about John is the fact that he was sent from God on a definite mission for a specific purpose. His mission was to bear witness of Jesus, the True Light, in order that men might believe in that Light, because of John's witness. John himself was a lesser light bearing witness of the True Light that came into the world to light the path of every man. Jesus said that John was a burning and shining light and that for a season men rejoiced in the light of John's true witness concerning Jesus. But John knew that the light that was in him and his witness was as a fluttering candle in the presence of the "Day-spring from on high." John said, "He must increase, but I must decrease." John knew that he was sent to be a witness and that Jesus was sent to be the Saviour, "the Lamb of God that taketh away the sin of the world." He realized the greatness of the difference between a mere witness and the mighty Saviour. But that did not keep him from bearing an effective witness. He magnified his mission. He glorified his office. He died as a martyr to the truth.

Now all of these truths concerning John the Baptist bring us face to face with the sobering fact that the true followers of Christ are sent, are called, are commissioned to be witnesses for him. He is on trial. We are called as witnesses, not as

29

lawyers to argue the case before an unfriendly jury. A witness is called because he or she is supposed to have first-hand, personal knowledge, pertinent to the case before the court. The witness is sworn to tell the truth, the whole truth, and nothing but the truth. Hearsay evidence is not admissible. It must be what the witness knows from personal observation or experience.

Unsaved people do not believe that Jesus was what he claimed to be, the Son of God, the one and only Saviour, able to save unto the uttermost them that draw near unto God through him. They do not believe that Jesus died on the Cross to make atonement for their sins. They do not believe that he arose from the dead, ascended into heaven and ever liveth to make intercession for those whom he has saved.

What do you know about Jesus? Do you know that he is the Saviour because he has saved you? Has he given you a sense of pardon, peace and power? Has he changed your life in any way? Has he helped you to face life's problems and trials with hopeful courage? Has he caused you to hate the evil and love the good? Can you truthfully say, "I know him in whom I have believed and am persuaded that he is able to keep that which I have committed unto him"?

If you can truthfully answer these questions in the affirmative with your lips then you are qualified to be an effective witness, and by all means you should bear your testimony. But I want to remind you that the testimony of your character and your record can be more powerful and convincing than the testimony of your lips. As a matter of fact, people will form their opinions of Christ from what you are, more than from what you say about him.

You, perhaps, are familiar with the old saying that the Christian is the world's Bible. Worldly people do not do much reading of the Bible, the written Word of God; but they do much reading of the lives of professed Christians. It is a blessed condition when the testimony of a Christian's lips and of a Christian's life are in perfect agreement. On the other hand, it is a tragic condition when one can say to a Christian, "What you are speaks so loudly that I cannot hear what you say."

Oh, my fellow Christians, we are all witnesses for Christ. We are either good witnesses or bad witnesses for him. We are good witnesses if our words, our deeds and our characters help people to believe in Christ. We are bad witnesses if what we say, what we do, and what we are, make it harder for people to believe in Christ and yield themselves unto him.

In one of the books of E. P. Roe, the story is told of a minister who faithfully and long sought to lead a worldly, skeptical young woman to Christ. He bore a good witness, better than he knew. She was cynical and indifferent, or so it seemed. The conditions surrounding her were altogether unfavorable to her becoming a Christian. The minister continued his verbal witness to Christ until the time came for him to be transferred to another field of labor. He went to tell the young woman goodbye and made a final appeal for her to believe in and accept Christ as her Saviour, apparently without result. But as he started to leave the girl burst into tears and said through her sobs, "I can believe on Jesus Christ because I can believe in you. I do believe in Christ, because I believe in you. Because of your testimony and your life I am able to believe in Christ. You are real, and because of your reality I can believe that Jesus about whom you talk is real."

Could that young woman possibly have paid that minister a higher tribute?

A few years ago there died in Waco, Texas, a good man, Mr. F. L. Carroll, whose memory will be held in loving esteem by all who knew him. Soon after Mr. Carroll's death, a citizen of that city, who was not a converted man at that time, said to me, "We fellows who have no connection with the churches have been discussing Mr. Carroll in our groups, and hundreds of us in Waco are obliged to believe in the gospel of Christ because Mr. Carroll exemplified its principles in his life."

Oh, my dear friends, when you have finished life's little day will people be able to say that because of your witness they were led to believe in Christ and his gospel? They can say that, and they will say that, if the witness of what you say and what you do and what you are, is the witness that it ought to be, and can be, with the help of Christ who said, "Lo: I am with you always."

CHAPTER III

Obeying the Master

C H A P T E R   I I I

Obeying the Master

His mother saith unto the servants,
Whatsoever he saith unto you, do it.
                                            —JOHN 2:5

I⊤ HAS deep significance that Christ's first miracle was performed at a wedding. If you or I had been asked what miracle would have been most appropriate to set at the front, at the beginning, of Christ's earthly ministry, I doubt if we would have chosen this miracle, this quiet, modest, beautiful miracle. Perhaps some of us would have put as the first miracle appropriate for him the raising of Lazarus. Or we might have selected the calming of the storm with just a word. Or we might have chosen as the first miracle the feeding of five thousand. It is significant that the Master chose as the time and place for his first miracle the wedding occasion. How he did hallow the home! How he did glorify the ties that bind a family together! He came to the chief institution in the social order, making for the welfare both of church and state when he hallowed the home. Everything is gone when the home is gone, and everything is conserved when we have the right kind of home. If the marriage relation be linked with Jesus all is well. If men flout the teaching of Jesus concerning the marriage relation, the result will be such as to make angels veil their faces. Jesus came to glorify our common, everyday life, and he would have us link it with him. He came to give gladness, and to turn vexation and disappointment and grief into joy and peace. He came to give our clouds a silver lining. He came to set the birds to singing. "Be of good cheer. I have overcome the world."

Trust me, and follow me, and all shall be well. That is the message of Jesus.

It is significant in this story that Jesus answered his mother as he did, when she told him that the wine had given out. What confidence Mary had in Jesus! She had long been pondering certain things in her heart, and she believed in his power to meet any exigency that should arise, and she ventured to say to him, "They have no wine," meaning also to suggest, "You will adjust that. You can." Jesus' answer to her seems abrupt. It was not. He sought to remind her that his orders were to come from his heavenly Father rather than from his earthly Mother. I believe that is what he meant when he said: "Woman, what have I to do with thee? Mine hour is not yet come."

In that statement Jesus refuted the doctrine that Mary is to be worshipped. There is not a falser heresy in the world than that the mother of Jesus is to be worshipped. She is not any more to be worshipped than your mother or mine. She is not a mediatrix. She is not the queen of heaven that some people say she is. Mary was just the plain mother of Jesus, a plain gracious woman, not to be worshipped at all, not to be prayed unto at all. The doctrine of Mariolatry abroad in the earth is to the last degree mischievous. "I am the way, the truth, and the life. No man cometh unto the Father but by me." "I am the door. By me, if any one enter in, he shall be saved." "Neither is there salvation in any other: for there is none other name under heaven given among men, whereby we must be saved." Jesus in his behaviour here gives marvellous emphasis to that truth.

But the words which Mary spoke to the servants are deeply meaningful words. "Whatsoever he saith unto you, do it." She recognized Jesus' right to absolute obedience from us all, and urged that such obedience be given by us all. The supreme need of every human being is to obey. The absolute need of every human being is to have a master to obey.

Let obedience be thrown away anywhere, and chaos will follow. What is a home where there is no obedience? My attention was brought to a case the past week; and when I saw how the children instead of the parents ran the house, I knew immediately why the house was in chaos. Children in the home are not to control it. The parents are to control it, and if they forget that, they are piling up wrath against the day of wrath. A home without proper parental control is a travesty of a home, and the same truth applies everywhere in the social order. What is a school wherein discipline and obedience are not magnified?

The saddest story back in the days of Israel is stated for us in one sentence: "In those days there was no king in Israel, and every man did that which was right in his own eyes." The well-being of society demands a standard of ethics, a standard of authority. The first and absolute and highest need of a human being is mastership of the right kind, control, obedience, in the right way. What would an army be without obedience, and where would an army get if the commands of superior officers were turned from and dawdled over and flagrantly set aside? The supreme need in human life ever is obedience, and the supreme need in the Christian life is obedience to Christ. A man's Christian life is a tame, tepid, wretched thing, if he does not understand: "Jesus is absolute master, and he has absolute right to every breath of my body, and to every deed of my hand, and to every thought of my life, and to the affection of my heart. He has the threefold right to it: He made me. He died for me. He preserves me. By this threefold right Jesus has absolute right to my constant and highest obedience."

So when Mary said to the servants, "Whatsoever Jesus says unto you, do it," she stated the great basic principle which runs through the Christian life. Note that she advised the servants to obey Christ literally, utterly, "Whatsoever he saith unto you, do it." What about that obedience? It is to be a personal obedience. No proxyship is there to be in religion, no deputyship in religion, no sponsorship in religion. Whether anybody else does right or not, you must. Whether anybody else lives up to a correct standard, you must.

If you consult Jonathan Edwards' diary—find it, if you can, and read it, one of the quaintest and most inspirational diaries any man has left for the after generations to read— you will come across this double resolution: "Resolved, first, that every man ought to obey Christ without any hesitation or reserve. Resolved, second, whether anybody else does or not, I will, so help me God." That is exactly correct. Whether anybody else does his duty or not, whether anybody else is vital and virile in devotion to Christ, whether anybody is punctual and conscientious in service for Christ or not, I must be. "Whatsoever he saith unto you, do it." Mary spoke better than she knew that day.

And then this obedience is to be a practical obedience. "Whatsoever he saith unto you, *do it*." Don't talk about it. Don't argue about it. Don't wonder about what will be the outcome. Don't speculate on the results. Don't cavil. "Whatsoever he saith unto you, do it." Surely that is the word that Christianity everywhere needs this hour. "Whatsoever Christ saith unto you, do it." Men come and ask me, "Why do you teach that, and why do you teach this?" and I have but one answer to give, "It is the clear teaching of Christ." Whatsoever Christ saith unto you, do that, and do that without reserve, and do that without any stint or waiting. Do what Christ says!

Great old John Wesley had many quaint sayings. One of the saints of the world was he. He had one saying to his preachers, wonderfully suggestive: "I did not give you these rules to mend them, but to mind them." "Whatsoever Christ saith unto you, do it." Now that is the way we are to serve Christ. Let a man halt and wait and falter at that point, and his Christian life will be wounded and maimed. Wellington had a great way of saying, "A man will never be fit to command others until he first himself learns how to obey implicitly and utterly."

Then you will notice that this obedience is to be universal. "Whatsoever Christ saith unto you, do it"—*whatsoever*. Sometimes I hear a man talking about "non-essentials" as he discusses the teachings of Christ. Non-essentials in the teachings of Christ! A man is in an alarming plight who can use language like that concerning the teachings of Christ. "Whatsoever Christ saith unto you, do it."

I dealt with a man recently who said, "I cannot for the life of me see the slightest significance in being baptized or in partaking of the Lord's Supper." The two great monuments Christ has set in his church are the Lord's Supper and baptism, and these monuments speak to the millions as the centuries come and go. There is that bread and there is that wine, and we ask what they mean, and are advised promptly. The bread sets forth in symbol the broken body of the Lord Jesus Christ, and the wine sets forth pictorially the poured out blood of Jesus. Baptism symbolizes his burial and his resurrection. How significant it is! Now, think of a man's temper of mind when he talks about the two great monuments in Christ's church being ignored or changed. They come with their marvellous meaning, and they proclaim louder than the voices of many waters before the millions of earth that Jesus, who was crucified and poured out his blood unto death for men, was buried in Joseph's new tomb, rose therefrom, victor over death and the grave.

"Whatsoever Christ saith unto you, do it." You and I are not to choose and cavil and select about this, or that, or the other saying of Jesus. You might as well talk abut changing the doctor's difficult prescription put there with the druggist. The druggist might as well say, "I will leave this out, and I will leave that other ingredient out, and mine will do as well as that, or even better." You can imagine the chaos

that would come to our health if men in the drug stores
trifled like that with the authorized prescriptions of those in
position to give them.

Whatsoever Christ saith unto you, do that. And do it joyfully. Do it in a great spirit. One volunteer is worth twenty
pressed men, so the old adage tells us. In a great spirit, not in
a craven, cringing spirit; in a joyful spirit go out to do just
what Christ bids you to do. The spirit makes a state. One
of the great things about our commonwealth is its great state
spirit. A city ought to have a great spirit, and every great
cause in it ought to have every man's enthusiastic support.
The greatest thing about a state or a city or a church or a
man is the spirit attaching to same. Now Jesus says to his
servants, to his friends, "I want you to do without delay, without cavil, I want you to do in a great spirit, everything I tell
you to do, and leave the rest with me." That is the advice
Jesus' mother gave to the servants, and it has passed down to
us.

Now, what comes from obedience to Christ? What follows
the right kind of obedience to Christ? Why should we obey
Christ like that? I have already said we should obey him
because we must obey somebody or something. The man
who talks about not having any master over him has the
basest and most despicable sort of a master. A man went up
and down this country some years ago prating against the
Bible and the church and Christianity, laughing at our authority claimed for Jesus, and he began one of his addresses
by saying, "So and so, and so and so, and so and so is my
religion." He had his master; he had his authority; he had
his lodestar. Every man must have some master. It may be his
money. What a master a man has when it is his money! "He
shall pierce himself through with many sorrows," the Bible
tells us, if a man's master is his money. It may be fashion.
It may be public opinion. Many a man through fear of others
betrays the highest and takes the downward plunge. It may

be pleasure, sparkling pleasure, consuming like the fire consumes the grass. It may be some base lust, that drags a man down from the highest hills and keeps him in the miasmatic swamps of folly and sin. Every man has some sort of master. It may be the devil, with all his wiles and wicked ways, who may be the master. Every man has a master.

Jesus comes, saying, "I, the Saviour and the Guide of mankind, would do everybody good, and no one evil at all, and I ask for your consent, not only to change you and forgive you and save you, but to guide you, and company with you and keep you on my road, forever." How glorious when the human spirit answers back, "That is the road for me, and I am going that road, without cavil or parleying."

We are to obey Jesus because he is the rightful Master. Worthy is he of all obedience. Worthy is he of all response from us. We think how worthy the national call for country, the national call for defenders of native land, and for defenders of principles dearer to mankind than human life itself, and we say, "That is well and good." Now, when we pass up to the highest realm of all, Jesus tells us, "I am supremely worthy, and I will confer upon you supremely worthy results, if I may have your unalloyed and unhesitating obedience." And when we give that kind of obedience, then the results are inexpressibly blessed. Oh, for a man to have singing within him the inner consciousness, "I did the best I could, what my Master bade me do!" There is a peace about it that passeth all understanding.

I told you years ago of a wreck when some of us returned from one of our conventions in the East. The train was divided into two parts in the Mississippi valley because of the great floods that overflowed the valley. The conductor on one of those trains at last lost patience because the train dragged on so slowly and time lost in the schedules was so great. At one little station the station keeper came out and said, "Here are orders for this passenger train to wait right here until a certain freight train up the road shall pass." But the conductor was out of patience and said, "I will make a certain switch yonder some miles away and have that much gained." The station keeper said, "Here are your orders. Here are the directions to hold this train until that great freight shall pass." And the conductor disobeyed and told the engineer to pull the throttle and to go with all speed for a certain switch a few miles away. The train thundered along with terrible speed over the iron tracks, and started up a hill, when lo, yonder, in sight, coming down that hill, was that vastly loaded freight train. What was to be done? Not a thing in the world. except to take the consequences. The two trains came together with a crash that fairly shook the hills, and then the dead were on every side. The freight conductor walked up and down in the midst of that wreck and debris, and amidst the wounded and the dying and the dead he took out of his pocket a little, soiled paper—it was his orders—and, crying like a child, said to the dead and to the dying, "Oh, I am not to blame! I obeyed orders. Here they are." But the conductor who disobeyed his orders had fled into the forest and could not face the situation. Oh, blessed beyond words, for us to do just what Jesus, our one infinitely wise and rightful Master tells us to do and then leave the results with him.

Jesus is to be obeyed literally, utterly, joyfully, always. That is the truth which the world needs to hear in every realm this hour. Men ask me, "Since Jesus Christ has infinite power, why does he not stop wars?" My answer is that if men had obeyed the golden rule, "Do unto others as you would have others do unto you," there would never have been a war, and peace would have smiled on every land and on every home in all the world.

There would never have been a war if men had not disobeyed the clear word of Jesus. The starting of armed conflicts is not a part of Christ's program. Just the reverse is true. If only men would do his bidding then they would "beat their swords into plough-shares, and their spears into pruning hooks; nation would not lift up sword against nation," nor would they learn war any more.

But this prophetic vision of Isaiah is far from realization in the world in which we live. Will it ever be realized? Yes, it will, when the peoples of the nations of the earth learn to obey the Son of God and put into practice the teachings of his gospel, and not before.

This solemn truth places a tremendous responsibility on all the friends and followers of Christ. So many millions know neither Christ nor his gospel. And they will never know him unless his followers obey him and to the limit of their ability seek to carry out his Great Commission.

There must be absolutely new adjustments for Christian people. They must face Jesus Christ and his task as they never faced it before. They must put him first, not talk about it, nor theorize, but do it. They must put Christ first in the courthouse, in the editor's sanctum, in the bank, in the store, in the shop, on the farm, everywhere. We must put Christ first, or the days ahead of us will fill the world with woes too deep for human speech and for human tears.

The only hope of this world is the Christian religion. The only hope of politics is the Christian religion. The only hope of business is the Christian religion. The only hope of society is the Christian religion. The only hope of the human soul, personally and individually, is the Christian religion.

> *My hope is built on nothing less*
> *Than Jesus' blood and righteousness;*
> *I dare not trust the sweetest frame,*
> *But wholly lean on Jesus' Name.*

CHAPTER IV

The Temptation of Our Saviour

The Tempation of Our Saviour

~~~~~~

Then was Jesus led up of the Spirit into the wilderness to be tempted of the devil.

—MATTHEW 4:1

THE TEMPTATION of Jesus was not a visionary one; it was a real one. He was tempted in all points like as we are, yet without sin. The only difference between his experience and ours is that we yield often to temptation, while he yielded never. It behooved him to be thus tempted, so that in all respects he would be touched with the feeling of our infirmities; and now no temptation that comes to man is beyond his appreciation and sympathy and help.

It is significant that the temptation of Jesus followed his baptism immediately. During that wonderful baptismal scene the heavens were opened, and the Holy Spirit descended like a dove and lighted upon him, and from the heavens there came a voice which said, "This is my beloved Son, in whom I am well pleased." How swift and surprising are the mutations of human experience! Just after the heavenly proclamation that he is God's Son, immediately came this sore temptation. Well did a great preacher say, "Do not question the validity of your baptism because it was succeeded by a fierce temptation." That is often true. Triumph is often followed by trial instantly. The hour of exaltation is very often succeeded immediately by the hour of humiliation and trial. The wondrous voice from out the clouds, the heavenly voice, is often succeeded by the voice from beneath, the voice from the pit. Blessed shall it be for us to remember this,

47

and then shall we know that our sonship with God is not dependent upon the rapidly varying moods of our earthly experience.

You will note that this trial of Jesus was not an accident. See the text, "Then was Jesus led up of the Spirit into the wilderness to be tempted of the devil." "Led up to be tempted—that is not an accident. There is purpose in that. Christ's temptations were not accidental, but they were all included in the great purpose which God had respecting the life and sufferings and death of his Son. "Led up of the Spirit into the wilderness to be tempted of the devil." That is the language. I grant you that there is deep mystery in it, and yet the great truth still abides that God's purpose pours through it all. Take away from life the thought of its education, and you have destroyed the deep meaning of human life. "Led up of the Spirit to be tempted of the devil."

That is the strange language, and yet the Scriptures show that thought all through their ever unfolding revelations. Not that man is solicited of God to do evil. Never! "Let no man say when he is tempted, I am tempted of God; for God cannot be tempted with evil, neither tempteth he any man." In no instance is man ever tempted of God to do evil, but in many instances, yea, in the instance of the life of every child of God, every one is subjected to trial, to discipline, to education. Do not the Scriptures clearly show that in the long ago God did tempt Abraham? That is, he tried him; he put him to the test. He subjected him to a process af self-examination and education that more than any other experience would strengthen his character. Understand, then, that trial is an essential part of God's great program for our lives. "Beloved, think it not strange concerning the fiery trial which is to try you, as though some strange thing happened unto you; but rejoice, inasmuch as ye are partakers of Christ's sufferings."

48

You notice that the Spirit of God here led Jesus "into the wilderness" to have his sore conflict. How often that is the case! Was it not so with Moses for forty long years? If Moses was to formulate the great principles of law and education and religion that were forever to dominate the world's thought and largely shape its life, it was needful that he spend forty years in the wilderness. Likewise also for a season must the wilderness be the home of Elijah. It must needs be true also of John the Baptist, who was to preach repentance as none other ever did preach it, save the Lord. And so of Paul, if he was to be earth's first apostle, he must spend three years in the quiet of Arabia. If Bunyan was to write an allegory that should be unmatched and forever matchless, he needed the twelve years' imprisonment of Bedford jail. If Milton was to write a poem that has no peer of its kind, he must know the isolation that came to him from blindness and other sore trials. All these wondrous workers must needs be taken into the wilderness, to have a trial, to have a testing time, to go through the discipline of training that the wilderness alone can give them.

My brethren, one danger of this age is that people live too much in crowds. No man shall ever come to the highest mark as a thinker and useful worker who lives always in the crowd. We have our magnificent systems of education, and our myriad inventions for the saving of labor and for adding to man's convenience; we have the great system of news-gathering that dumps all the news of this planet down at our doors every morning and every evening; and thus, it is to be feared, we are getting away from the race of the world's great thinkers, because we are not led often enough to the wilderness, that there, single handed and alone, we may think out and fight out some of the deep battles of the inner life.

Let us look at these three temptations that came to Jesus in the wilderness. These three comprehend every possible temptation that ever comes to mankind. First, there was the

49

temptation through the body. After forty days and forty nights of fasting, Jesus was an hungered. For days and nights he was miraculously sustained. His human body felt the sense of hunger. Just then the devil appeared. Oh, he is an errant coward. There is not a thing brave about the devil. He is always sinuous and slimy and cowardly. He never did a courageous thing in his life. Now, when the humanity of Jesus was put to its sorest test, the shrewd, cowardly imp of the pit appeared and appealed with a temptation to Jesus' hungry body.

What was that temptation? Yielding to it would have meant what? The yielding to it on the part of Jesus would have meant distrust of his Father. Satan said to him, "Why, you are hungry. Make bread out of rocks. Turn these stones into food. A hungry man ought to eat." Jesus could have done it, but to have yielded to that temptation would have been to show forth absolute distrust of his Father and utterly discard his guardianship and protection. And so Jesus hurled back at the tempter the sublime statement, "It is written, Man shall not live by bread alone, but by every word that proceedeth out of the mouth of God." Christ here says that his Father does not have to turn the rocks into bread in order to sustain the life of his Son. He can preserve life otherwise. Bread is not the main thing in a man's life. God's Word, proceeding out of his mouth, is far more worthy and helpful than mere earthly bread. Christ would yield not to the seductive tempter. He would trust his Father whose providential love would in no wise fail him.

That is a piercing temptation to which all men are subjected, the temptation that comes to the body. By that temptation Adam and Eve were led to fall. The temptation began with an appeal to the body. With subtle voice the tempter whispered, "The tree is good for food, and it is pleasant to the eyes, and it is a tree to be desired to make one wise," and by this time Eve was ready to eat of the

50

fruit and to give also unto her husband; and even thus was brought to pass the fall and ruin of the race. The temptation of the body, its name is legion. There is selfishness, appealing to us on the one hand with its manifold expressions. There is appetite, pulling and tugging at the very vitals of our life every day. There is indolence, that rocks us and soothes us, and continually whispers to us sweet things about the welfare and comfort of our dear bodies. Appetite in all its forms unceasingly knocks at the door of our hearts and talks about the necessity of our eating this particular food and doing this particular thing. Well might Paul cry out, "Who shall deliver me from the body of this death?" Very many of the sorest temptations of life come through the body. This one appealed to Jesus through his body, but victoriously he met it, and completely foiled the tempter.

Then the tempter approached our Lord again from an utterly different standpoint. He took him up into the holy city, and set him on a pinnacle of the temple, and made to him this remarkable statement: "Cast thyself down, for it is written, he shall give his angels charge concerning thee, and in their hands they shall bear thee up, lest at any time thou dash thy foot against a stone." Do you see how sly it was? This is wonderful for the devil to be quoting Scripture, but he quotes it here just as he always quotes it. He does not quote it correctly. What he says here does sound like Scripture, but he leaves out the salient point. Here is what he said to the Master: "Cast thyself down; for it is written, he shall give his angels charge concerning thee." Satan failed to quote all the sentence. He left out a few words that were the key to all of it. These were the words left out: "To keep thee in all thy ways." That is to say, God will keep thee in thy rightful ways, in thine appointed ways, in God's providential ways, in the ways marked out by his own infinite wisdom and love. He will keep thee in these ways, but the devil left all

51

that qualifying condition out; he omitted the vital point of the Scripture.

This is a subtle temptation indeed. Do you see its cunning and audacity? It is nothing short of an appeal to Christ to experiment upon the purpose and power of God, and to force meanings into his promises wholly foreign to the intention of his Spirit, and to put God into a situation forbidden both by his Word and nature. Its meaning broadly interpreted is, let man do what he wills, however careless or wilful or self-risking it may be. God is pledged to keep him. Criminally sad is this wresting of the divine promises. Just here even many a Christian stumbles to his great shame and harm. He shuts his eyes and presumes upon God. Have you not seen it a hundred times? Men thus trifle with health, with character, with evil influences. They dwell upon their own great strength, they write down strong resolutions, they pray; but they turn from all these into presumptuous sins. God has a plan and limit and purpose and boundary in all that he says and does. He never anywhere says that his child shall be safely upheld if he presumes to cast himself down from the pinnacle of the temple. Only does he promise to keep his children in lawful ways; but they must not presume to dally with danger and say, God will keep me; nor to go forth into sin, saying, grace will abound.

You will also notice that the devil here talked about "angels." "Cast thyself down, and he shall give his angels charge concerning thee." Yea, he talked glibly about "angels." You have heard some men talk with a degree of seeming familiarity with God and his Word, and yet the trend of their lives stamps them as the enemies of the cross of Christ. The devil quoted Scripture and talked about angels and all that, and yet he was the adversary, the seducer, the old dragon of the pit. Quoting Scripture does not mean that a man is in fellowship with God. Talking about angels does not mean that a man has any sort of kinship to them. Jesus repelled this temptation as he did the other, and the devil was hurled into defeat again.

And now Satan came the third time, and this time he took Jesus up on a high mountain, and showed him all of the kingdoms of the world and the glory of them, and then he made to Jesus this proposal: "If you will fall down and worship me, I will give them all to you." Unparalleled impudence! Unbridled presumption! Not a solitary inch of any of these kingdoms did the devil own, not one has he ever owned, and not one shall he ever own. To be sure he is here, but he is an intruder here. He is on property that is not his own, and it is the business of the redeemed of God while they abide on the earth to contest every inch of the ground with this personal devil. Nor shall our work be done below until the whole earth be redeemed to God. There is a personal devil operating among men, seeking ever to influence and destroy them, just as literally as there is a personal God seeking to redeem and save. The denial of this proposition is the baldest infidelity. But suppose the devil had had all those kingdoms of the world that he declaimed about. Suppose they had been his, for argument's sake. Could the Lord have yielded to his proposal? Nay, never; it would have meant instant dethronement of the Almighty. It would have been the instant annihilation of the kingdom of righteousness.

What is this proposal here? It is substantially this: The devil said, "Saviour, Messiah, Son of God, I have a proposal to make to you. You have three years yet to live. You have just been baptized. You have three years in which to preach and suffer, and to be scourged, and to be wounded in heart, both by your enemies and friends, and at the end to die on the shameful tree of the cross. You have all that ahead of you. Suppose you and I go into partnership. You bow down and say just one prayer to me, and I will make you a title deed to all of this business. Let us go into partnership. Let us have an amalgamation of heaven and hell. Let us have a compromise of the two great establishments upon mutual terms, and then the lion and the lamb will lie down side by side, and the devil and God will be twin brothers, and there will be no conflict at all. That means for you, O Jesus, no humiliation, no weariness, nor pain, nor conflict with all the complexities and difficulties of your plan of salvation. And it also means for you, O Jesus, no betrayal, no dark Gethsemane, no Calvary and no death. Take a nearer route to rulership. Just make one concession to Satan, and he will vacate the field and you shall have it all your own way." That, in effect, was Satan's proposal in that awful hour.

Is there anywhere any possible amalgamation of the principles of righteousness with the principles of unrighteousness? Nay, never; it cannot be. If Jesus had that day bowed before Satan and said, "I will say one prayer unto thee, O Satan, for just one minute," the kingdom of righteousness would have been forever annihilated that same minute. That momentary compromise would have meant defeat eternal to the kingdom of God. There is not to be a scintilla of compromise between the kingdom of evil and the kingdom of righteousness. Any pandering to any of the principles of the kingdom of evil is but a yielding to this subtle seduction and temptation of the devil when he asked Christ on the mountain to give him one moment's concession and worship. That moment would have meant eternal treason to truth, to righteousness, and to God. There is not one inch of room for pretense or double dealing in the kingdom of God.

Every questionable method in Christ's church of any shape, form, or fashion is but the pandering to the kingdom of evil and the yielding to this third temptation that came to Christ. It is the same old suggestion that so often we hear, "Let us do evil that good may come." Every such policy is the palpable and fundamental violation and subversion of every principle inculcated by God's Word. I do not hesitate to say that if Christ's praying one prayer unto Satan that day would have won all the world, he could not have made such concession. A salvation so effected would have been no salvation at all. The Lord, he is God, and to him alone shall be given homage and worship. For Jesus to have made one concession would have been the utter annihilation of his own righteous character, and his own rightful authority over the children of men.

You must not do evil that good may come. If, by the doing of some present evil, you think you can see good out there in the distance, you are not to do it. You are not allowed to do evil whatever the allurement or harvest promised. That is identically what Satan here proposed: "O Christ, do a little evil, and I will get off the ground! Say one prayer to me, and I will vacate the whole territory." But the Lord held out in the conflict steadily against Satan, and repelled him a third time with the wondrous sentences of his Father's Word. Somebody has suggestively said that "Of all the essences that the devil likes, he best likes acquiescence." "Resist the devil, and he will flee from you." And the supreme weapon for such resistance is that same conquering one used by Christ: "It is written." In all your conflicts with temptation, O Christian, take "the sword of the Spirit which is the Word of God."

Did you ever notice where the Lord got all these quotations? He got them from the book of Deuteronomy. I have not a doubt that our Lord knew that many centuries later certain clever little men would be trying to destroy this book of Deuteronomy. The Divine Son of God, looking down through the ages, saw the coming conflict, and he got these quotations out of the book he knew would be so vehemently attacked.

But now, after these three conflicts with the tempter what became of the Saviour? The devil was completely routed; but what of the Saviour? Here is the answer: "Behold, angels came and ministered unto him." All during that dreadful conflict, lingering near by, the angels of God watched the awful struggle, the Son of God did meet in the open field the dark fiend of the pit, and contest with him every inch of the ground. And now, when the devil was baffled, defeated and driven away, the "angels came and ministered unto Jesus." Thus it is evermore.

When Jesus prayed in Gethsemane that last awful night, before he took up the march to the cross, saying, "Nevertheless, not my will, but thine be done," "an angel appeared unto him from heaven, strengthening him." The angels, doubtless, are spectators in all our conflicts with the temptations of life: "The angel of the Lord encampeth round about them that fear him, and delivereth them."

What is the outstanding lesson today for us in all this story of Jesus' temptation? The lesson is for us to hold on to the right, ever repelling the tempter with this sure weapon which our Lord used—"It is written." Oh, be not misled and overcome by the old fiend of the pit. Evermore stand on the Word of God, and here shall you find rest and victory for your souls.

There are two plans whereby men may resist temptation. The one has been called "the plan of resistance," the other "the plan of counter-attraction." Both are illustrated from stories in Greek mythology. The one finds illustration in the story of the Greeks who must sail by the island of the sirens as they return from Troy. Bewitching strains of music came to the Greeks as they neared the island, so that they were seized with the desire to throw themselves into the sea and swim to the sirens. But this would have meant their certain and speedy death, and for this alone the treacherous sirens sang their enchanting songs. Then the leader made the Greeks to fill their ears with wax, and had himself bound thoroughly to the boat so that when they passed the shore where the sirens dwelt and they should begin their strains of entrancing music, the men with stopped ears could not hear, and the leader, though he should wish to go, would be bound hand and foot so that he could not; and thus they could make the journey in safety. This is the method of resistance, but that method is not the best.

The other story illustrates the other method, the method of counter-attraction. It is the story of the Argonauts, who sailed with Jason in search of the golden fleece, and they also had to round that same island, where sang the sirens. They took on board with them Orpheus, whose music entranced the very beasts of the forests, and made even the trees to wave before him in homage. As they came where the sirens dwelt, and as the sirens began to play the soft music, Orpheus struck the wondrous notes of his lyre, so that all the air vibrated with the sweet melodies, and all the sailors on the boat laughed to scorn the sirens, and the voyagers rounded the shore in safety. That is the method whereby you and I are to overcome temptation in the experiences of our earthly life. This alone is the sure way of triumph. "This I say, then, 'walk in the spirit,' and ye shall not fulfil the lusts of the flesh." "Ye shall know the truth, and the truth shall make you free." "If the Son shall make you free, you shall be free, indeed."

O my wearied, battling, tempted friends, whether saved or lost, freely and fully admit Jesus into your heart and life, and then shall you overcome. And know that if left to your own poor strength you will surely go down before temptation's power. Will you not heed his precious call today? It is this: "Behold, I stand at the door and knock; if any man hear my voice, and open the door, I will come to him, and will sup with him, and he with me." "And whosoever will, let him take the water of life freely." Come to him now. Cast yourself utterly and forever upon him, and you shall find rest for your soul.

CHAPTER V

The Value of Temptations

C H A P T E R   V

The Value of Temptations

~~~~~~

> *Count it all joy when ye fall into manifold temptations.*
>
> —JAMES 1:12
>
> *Blessed is the man that endureth temptation.*
>
> —JAMES 1:2

THE MAN who made these startling statements was the half-brother of Jesus and the pastor of the church at Jerusalem. He knew whereof he spoke. For years he had disbelieved in Jesus and had scorned the claims of Jesus that he was the Son of God, the Messiah, the Saviour of the world. In so doing, James had yielded to the temptations of Satan, which temptations found congenial lodgement in the stubborn and self-righteous heart of James until after the resurrection of Jesus. We have good reason to believe that it was to this James that Jesus appeared after his resurrection (see I Cor. 15:7). It is evident that a great transformation took place in this James whom Paul called "the Lord's brother" (Gal. 1:19). He was acquainted with manifold testings, trials, temptations and knew the joy and the blessedness of the grace of God, which had enabled him to overcome them so that he could describe himself as "servant of God and of the Lord Jesus Christ" in the opening sentence of his epistle "to the twelve tribes which are scattered abroad."

One of the amazing things about the Bible is the utter frankness with which it describes human beings, even those who are called the heroes of faith and the saints of God. In this respect, the Bible may be likened unto a candid camera which faithfully portrays both good and bad features. A good camera does not lie, and neither does the Bible. A camera tells the truth even though it be embarrassing. Often we are embarrassed and shamed when we are shown the untouched negatives of ourselves. We had not realized that we are so homely.

The Bible is like a great mirror in which we can see ourselves as we really are physically. When one looks into the Bible mirror he can see what he is spiritually. And if he can be persuaded to compare that spiritual likeness of himself with the perfect portrait of the perfect Christ, the sinless God-man, the spotless Lamb of God that taketh away the sin of the world, the contrast is so great that he is humbled into the dust and is prompted to cry out, "God be merciful to me a sinner."

The Bible makes it very clear that all have sinned and come short of the glory of God. And that is because all have been subjected to temptations from within or from without, and all, in one way or another, have yielded to such temptations and gone down before them—all except Jesus. He like all the rest of humanity was subjected to temptation, but he alone of all humanity never yielded to temptation. He alone was without sin. That is one reason why he can help and save sinners. That is the meaning of the hymn we sometimes sing:

> Yield not to temptation,
> For yielding is sin;
> Each victory will help you
> Some other to win;
> Fight manfully onward,
> Dark passions subdue,
> Look ever to Jesus,
> He'll carry you through.

We are told that Jesus the Son of God, our high priest, was touched with the feeling of our infirmities and was tempted in all points, like as we are, yet he was without sin; and therefore we should draw near with boldness unto the throne of grace, that we may receive mercy, and find grace to help us in time of need.

We have every reason to believe that James had been a sorely tempted man and that he had often yielded to temptation; but because of Jesus he had boldly approached the throne of grace and had received pardoning mercy and saving and sustaining grace. Thus he had learned the possible values of manifold trials and temptations. If resisted, if endured, if overcome, temptations could be made stepping-stones to higher things, they could become the proof of one's faith, they could become the occasion for receiving the crown of life. This is the enheartening counsel concerning temptations which James wrote to his fellow Jews scattered abroad.

James was in complete harmony with the oft-repeated teachings of the Bible that there is strength in struggle, that there may be advantage in disadvantages, that to him who overcomes is promised the crown of life, that there may be great value in temptations. It behooves us to discover, if we can, some of these values, because we are subjected to so many temptations all our days.

The untried and untempted man would be ignorant of his own heart, his character, his powers, his strength and his weakness. Temptations disclose to us what we really are. They furnish us an opportunity to find out how weak and helpless we are, and how much we need divine help if we are to be victorious in life's battles. Often they drive us to the unfailing source of pardon, peace and power, even unto that One who alone is able to save unto the uttermost. Therefore none should think it strange that fiery trials should be permitted to come upon them along life's way.

James was careful to warn: "Let no man say when he is tempted, 'I am tempted of God'; for God can not be tempted with evil, and he himself tempteth no man: but each man is tempted, when he is drawn away by his own lust, and enticed." "Lust," as used here by James, means one's inherent evil nature.

God permits fiery trials to come upon us, but he is not the author of them. He does that for some beneficient purpose, which purpose may be hard for us to see at the time. But we may be assured that God is never the author of evil. Only good and perfect gifts come to us "from the Father of lights, with whom can be no variation, neither shadow that is cast by turning."

How little a man knows about himself until temptations come upon him and reveal what manner of man he is by the way he yields to or overcomes those temptations! Often they come upon us unawares. They spring upon us like wild beasts lurking beside a jungle path. When Solomon began his reign he was humble, devout, just and considerate. He soon won the reputation of being the wisest of men. But under the temptations incident to power, prosperity, popularity, great wealth and vaulting ambition he became a wretched voluptuary and one of the biggest fools and worst pessimists of all time. The stories of Saul, Israel's first king, Alexander the Great, Herod the Great, Rome's Nero, Scotland's "Bloody Mary" were much the same. They all began well, and they all ended as bloody tyrants who filled people with horror and became stenches in the nostrils of God. They did not endure temptation. They were not blessed, but cursed.

Simon Peter is a classical example of a man who bit the dust of humiliation before a sudden temptation. From the heights of professed loyalty he, within a few hours, descended to the depths of shameful lying and blasphemous denial of his Lord and Master. But, thank God, he is also a classical example of one, who, by divine help, climbed again to the heights of loyalty, even unto death. The oak tree never knows its strength until tested by the fiercest storm. The bridge across the stream never knows its strength until it is assailed by the raging floods.

Everyone has his or her own peculiar temptations. No one is exempt. The rich man has his manifold cares in the midst of his luxuries and plenty. The poor man has his many cares, anxieties, fears, distrusts and envyings. The good man has to guard against self-righteousness, over self-confidence, lack of sympathy for those whom he thinks are less good than himself, the temptation to sit in the seat of the scornful. A beautiful woman has to guard against vanity and trying to feed her soul upon the praise that comes from those around her. The homely woman must needs guard against envy and bitterness and jealousy and those other ranklings within her heart that tend to give her an inferiority complex.

As a rule, Satan tempts us at our weakest point. He seeks out a weak spot in our moral or spiritual character and makes his attack at that point. It is the same way with disease, that other enemy of our well-being. Disease searches out some weak place in the body and there gets in its deadly work. How careful we should be to fortify our known weak spots strongly!

Strange as it may seem, sometimes we are tempted and fail right at our strongest point. The instances are numerous, illustrative of this truth. It was so with Elijah. His strongest characteristic was his moral courage. He seemed almost god-like as he stood on Mount Carmel and hurled at the vicious priests of Baal defiance and biting sarcasm that drove them into a frenzy. Then with sublime faith and daring he called on God to vindicate himself and his prophet by sending fire from heaven to consume the altar and the sacrifice upon it. Then the fire fell and consumed it all. When we read the account of this mighty drama in the First Book of Kings our hearts are filled with pride that a member of the human family could be such a hero of faith and courage. And yet— and yet, within a day's time we see our hero fleeing far to the south because wicked Jezebel had threatened his life. He fled as a poltroon, a base coward, a very human weakling until, exhausted, he fell under a juniper tree and whimpered out his plea that he might die, because he was no better than his fathers. Elijah had failed at his strongest point. Had pride crept in? Who, other than Elijah, had thought that he was better than his fathers? Pride often goeth before a fall. We are not surprised that a great musician composed a powerful oratorio and called it *Elijah*.

John the Apostle, called "the beloved disciple," was another who on one occasion failed so seriously right at his strongest point that Jesus solemnly rebuked him. His strongest characteristic was his lovable and loving disposition. He loved people and he loved Jesus and Jesus loved him. I sometimes think that John loved Jesus more than any of the other apostles. Love is one of the main themes in John's five books in our New Testament. And yet, this same John of the loving heart was made so indignant by the inhospitality shown Jesus by a certain Samaritan village that he and his brother, James, asked Jesus if they might be allowed to command fire to come down from heaven and consume the people of that village. The vindictive spirit displayed by John and James under sudden provocation was doubtless the reason why Jesus gave these brothers a surname which meant "Sons of Thunder."

It is a great victory for Satan when he can successfully assail us at our strongest point, for then he hopes to capture the whole fortress of our hearts. If we are wise, we will guard our strong points as well as our weak points. For the enemy of our souls is persistent, relentless and exceedingly clever. He will destroy us if he can. We cannot resist him, defeat him, overcome him if we rely only on our own strength. We need and must have divine help if we are to be victorious. Under the tutelage of the Holy Spirit we must learn how to wield the sword of the Spirit which is the Word of God. Satan can always be routed by the sword of the Spirit in the hand of a true soldier of the cross.

Since all are subjected to temptations, some at their weakest points and others at their strongest points, and all are in danger of falling before such temptations, especially if they rely only on their own powers of resistance, it is highly important that all seek to avoid temptation. Jesus taught us to pray that we be not led into temptation. We are counselled to avoid meeting temptations, to go not in the way of dangerous testings, but to walk in the paths of righteousness. We are told: "He that walketh with wise men shall be wise, but the companion of fools shall be destroyed."

How foolish is the person whose thirst for strong drink is as a raging fire, if that person deliberately goes where he or she will be tempted by that deadly foe!

Why go near somebody who exercises over you a strange spell for evil? Why not avoid the harmful influence of that person as you would a deadly plague?

The counsel of divine wisdom is that we should avoid temptation, pass not down its ways, nor enter into its courts.

If we really desire to overcome evil temptations, then we should constantly seek to cultivate the consciousness of the presence of God. How could the murderer by night stealthily seek out his foe and take his life, if he could only realize that God's eyes were upon him? How could a man pursue his adulterous way if he understood that God knows all about it and condemns him as a vicious sinner? Oh, that all might have a consciousness of God's presence and God's all-seeing eye! Those who have such consciousness are the ones who can count it all joy even when they are assailed by many trials and testings for they endure and overcome temptations and are the truly blessed ones.

Do you recall the opening words of the first Psalm? "Blessed is the man that walketh not in the counsel of the ungodly, nor standeth in the way of sinners, nor sitteth in the seat of the scornful. But his delight is in the law of the Lord; and in his law doth he meditate day and night." That is the kind of man who can say "Thy word have I hid in my heart, that I might not sin against thee," for it is "a lamp unto my feet, and a light unto my path."

And the last word our Master gives us in order to meet temptation as we ought is that we be men and women of steadfast prayer. "Pray that ye enter not into temptation." "If any man lack wisdom let him ask of God." James was discussing temptation when he wrote that. If a man is tempted, and his difficulties are strangely complicated and he lacks wisdom, let him ask of God; let him pray; let him present his problem before the Holy One; let him flee to the great Divine Parent and put his case in his hands, and God will give him wisdom liberally, and God will not upbraid, and God will deliver.

O my friends, when trials and temptations come, treat them as they ought to be treated. Let them speak to you as the revelation of your own hearts, of the proneness of your own natures to do wrong, and because of such revelations flee unto the hills whence cometh your help. And by such revelations be taught humility, be taught charity, be taught absolute dependence upon God, who is our refuge and strength, a very present help in trouble.

CHAPTER VI

The Protest of Evil

C H A P T E R   V I

The Protest of Evil

Let us alone.

—MARK 1:24

JESUS was mighty both in word and in deed. This fact is illustrated in Mark's account of the healing of the demoniac. Both Mark and Luke introduce this narrative by telling us of the marvelous effect of the words which Jesus spoke to the people. As the people listened they were moved with astonishment by the power of what he was saying. The reason is given: "He spoke as one having authority, and not as the scribes."

The scribes dealt in subtleties, in hair-splitting discussions, in by-plays upon words, in subterfuges of speech. Here was one who spoke with authority. There was a note of authority in everything he said. There was a calmness and confidence in his speech different from anything the people had ever heard before. Jesus could thus speak because he was himself the truth, the incarnation of the truth which he taught.

There in Capernaum where he stood up to speak in the synagogue that sabbath day was a man with an unclean spirit, a man possessed with a demon. While Jesus was speaking in the matchless way which I have just indicated, the demon cried out, "Let us alone, what have we to do with thee, thou Jesus of Nazareth? Art thou come to destroy us? I know thee who thou art, the Holy One of God."

Then Jesus revealed his authority and his power in the midst of the people. He expelled the demon from the poor, driven, unfortunate man and set him free.

This incident of the healing of the demoniac furnishes us some simple yet profoundly practical lessons that I trust we may study today with profit.

The first lesson suggested in this incident is the protest that evil makes when confronted with righteousness. What is that protest? When Jesus began to speak in the synagogue words of truth and righteousness this demon cried out, "Let us alone, what have we to do with three, thou Jesus of Nazareth, let us alone." That is the protest of evil. That has been the protest of evil from the time that the first pair in the Garden of Eden were seduced and tried to hide from God. Let righteousness and evil face each other and the cry of evil in every case is, "Let us alone, what have we to do with thee, thou Jesus of Nazareth!"

That cry is heard early in life. Those of you who have babes at your homes have heard it, "Let us alone!" The little fellows, long before they can frame their speech, frame it with their fists, with their scowls, with their angry looks; and when they begin to talk their frequent insistence is that they shall be let alone to do as they please. When righteousness seeks to constrain and restrain our growing youths, the cry of evil which slumbers in their youthful hearts often is, "Let us alone." No one likes to be rebuked for his iniquities. Often when one is called in question, his feeling is, "I wish you would mind your own business." That is the protest of evil which slumbers in the human heart.

That protest is also the protest of public evil as well as of individual evil. "Let us alone, O church, what have we to do with thee? Let us alone, O preacher of the gospel, what have we to do with thee?" It is the cry of every public evil on the face of the earth. Let any attempt be made to deal with some social evil and from the mountains to the sea the protest will be, "Let us alone."

Whenever any protest is made by righteousness against an unrighteous law, the cry of the advocates of such law, loud and bitter and long, will be, "Let us alone." Whenever right-

eousness challenges the bad influences of any pernicious institution, the same cry that came from the lips of the unfortunate man of our text is repeated by the supporters of
that evil institution, "Let us alone, what have we to do with
you, and what have you to do with us; stay on your territory
and we will stay on ours. Let us alone!" That is the cry of
every public evil on the face of the earth, and always has
been. The protest of idolatry has ever been just that.

As God's people go out as witnesses for Jesus into China
and Africa and Asia and the rest of the earth to lift up the
standard of Jesus Christ, idolatry in every land cowers and
winces and cries out, "Let us alone. We do not want to be
disturbed. Go away with the light and hope and promise of
your gospel. We prefer darkness and superstition and ignorance." And alas! some people of evil spirit in so-called
Christian lands agree with the protest of the pagans and
say that Christians should not disturb the heathen religions
in foreign lands. That was what they said after the Boxer
uprising in China when so many Christian missionaries and
native converts were ruthlessly slaughtered. Numerous editors of great American newspapers said, "We ought to have
left them alone."

Take, for example, the highly organized and deeply in-
trenched liquor interests which, like some great octopus, seek
to entangle a whole nation in their poisonous tentacles. How
fierce and furious are their protests if and when the preachers
and churches and others of good will dare to raise their
voices in righteous indignation against the wicked, destructive and destroying influence of this vast social evil. The
protest of all connected with this social and political enemy of
all righteousness and truth and sobriety and decency and
morality and all true religion is ever, "Leave us alone; attend
to your own business and we will attend to ours."

And the same thing can be said of other great social evils
such as organized crime, condoned prostitution and gambling.
Can you imagine a greater folly than that displayed by cer-

tain religious bodies which not only permit but also sponsor gambling games on the church property and seek to justify it on the grounds that man inherently is a gambler? Yes, man is inherently evil, so much so that he is ever ready to protest against any check-mating of his evil doings. The universal cry of evil is the cry of that demon-possessed man in the synagogue at Capernaum, "Leave us alone!"

Now I want you to notice the two questions the demon within the man asked Jesus. They are: "What have we to do with thee, thou Jesus of Nazareth?" and: "Art thou come to destroy us?" Especially I want you to notice the "we" and the "us" in these questions. What did the unclean spirit, or the demon, in the man mean by using these plural personal pronouns? Evidently the demon meant that he had so fully entered and possessed and dominated the man that if he, the demon, were destroyed, the man also would be destroyed; he meant to say that there was complete identity between the man and the demon. He was saying, in effect, "This man and I know that you are Jesus of Nazareth, the Holy One of God; and surely you do not want to destroy this man, which you will surely do if you destroy me. I am making a plea for this man. I am his friend. He likes me and I like him. Just let us alone. We are doing all right." If that is what the demon meant, then he was uttering a lie that was conceived in the deepest pit of hell. Neither Satan nor his demons are ever the friends of those they dominate. They enter, they deceive, they bind, they destroy, they doom and damn their victims. Judas found out that truth too late.

Satan invades the realms of business and law and society and when righteousness raises its protest the cry is, "Art thou come to destroy us? Why you are a destroyer of business, of society, of law." Satan would represent himself as man's best friend. Mark you this, sin was never a friend to man's rights or man's safety or man's happiness—never, in any place in the world.

Jesus Christ, to be sure, came to destroy the works of the devil, but his purpose in destroying the works of the devil is to save devil-possessed men. The only way to save devil-driven men at all is to destroy the works of the devil which bind and delude and destroy men. When Jesus insists that business shall be honest, does that mean that he would destroy business? When he insists that social customs shall be chaste and pure, does that mean that he disapproves of the right kind of social custom? When he insists that man's reactions shall not be marred and spoiled by lust or gambling or some other evil, does that mean that he is an enemy of man? How utterly false is the plea that evil makes when it insists that evil is the friend of business and that religion is not!

This protest made by the demon at Capernaum was not only utterly false, but it was also utterly impudent. "Let us alone!" Now, what right had the demon to say that? It is the cry of the murderous gangster yonder on the streets, shooting right and left, leaving death and fear and a holocaust of destruction in his wake. When the majesty of the law seeks to restrain him his cry is, "Let us alone." Oh, when will the world learn the primary truth that evil has no rights at all? What right has sin? No right has sin on the earth unless this earth belongs to Satan, and it certainly does not. I know that he is here leading multitudes to destruction. But the business of Jesus and the hosts who love and follow him is to drive Satan and all his minions of evil from the face of the earth. Evil has not one right on the earth, not one. And that being true, the protests which Satan makes are not only false but utterly impudent.

Still further, the protest which the demon made to Jesus was not only false and impudent, but it was equally cruel. "Art thou come to destroy us? Let us alone!" At first glance that sounds like a plea for mercy. But when the crisis came, when that demon had to leave that man, expelled by the power of Jesus, he tore the man grievously and cried with a loud voice, and came out. Satan reveals himself, bye and bye, to

75

every man; but alas, in most instances his revelation is too late for a man to be saved.

What if Jesus had let the demon alone? The poor demon-possessed man would have been destroyed, both body and soul forever. And what if Christ's representatives, Christ's people on the earth, shall listen to the voice of evil, as from every side its blatant cry is, "Let us alone"? What if Christ's church were to do that? She would have no mission on earth, no place among the sons of men, no kinship to her divine Lord. Christ's church cannot let demons alone. Christ's church cannot be silent in the face of one bad law or one pernicious institution on the face of the earth. Christ's church would be cruel beyond measure to men if she were to let alone the evil and be seduced to quietness by its subtle protest.

Look about you and you will see a thousand evils about which Christ's church cannot be silent. Can you let alone your own children when the habits of selfishness and disobedience and intemperance and irreverence are fastening themselves upon your children? If so, you are utterly unworthy to be their parents. Jesus said, "I came to destroy the works of the devil." Can Christ's church take a different attitude from her divine Lord and be silent in the face of evils that delude and destroy the world? To do that would be to bring in the reign of moral and spiritual chaos.

Yonder in the back alley is a woman with three boys, seeking to bring them up in the nurture and admonition of the Lord, seeking to instill into them the principles of sobriety and integrity and righteousness, in all life's manifold relations. If you and I, by silent acquiescence, shall allow laws and pernicious institutions and customs to stretch out their baleful influences and get that woman's boys, then our cruelty to her and her sons cries to God for vengeance. And I now say to business men listening to me this morning that an incomparably bigger and better thing for this world's welfare than railroads or factories or banks is that woman's fight to bring up her boys in the nurture and admonition of the Lord. That woman is entitled to the moral support and practical helpfulness of every decent man and woman in the city where she lives.

But a moment more. Note how Jesus made answer to the protest of the demon. He said to him, "Hold thy peace and come out of that man," or literally translated, he said to the demon, "Be muzzled and come out of that man." Have you observed that there is not an instance on record of where Jesus ever argued with the devil? Never a time; never once. And we are in danger every time we try to argue with the devil. Jesus never in a single instance stopped to parley with evil; and never did he accept any favors from evil. Christ's church should follow his example in dealing with evil.

You remember the Trojans and Greeks of old. The Trojans dreaded to receive gifts from the Greeks, and well they might, for one day there came from the Greeks a wooden horse, and they said, "We have brought you a gift, the finest that ever was made. Open your gates and receive this wooden horse." The horse was accepted and installed within the walls of the city. But inside that horse were armed men. When night came on those men slipped quietly from their hiding place and threw the bolts of the gates which guarded the city and the enemy swarmed in. Christ's church, like her Lord, is never to listen for a moment to one doubtful compliment from any enemy that Christ has in the world.

Jesus said to this demon, "Be muzzled; don't open your mouth again; and come out of that man." And the Scripture tells us that with a loud voice the demon tore the man and came out of him. That is Satan's method generally—a loud voice. He greatly enjoys a big panic. But the demon came out.

You recall what Victor Hugo said about the battle of Waterloo. Men on the right hand and on the left were asking, "Who was responsible for the victory?" And Victor Hugo said "God won the battle." And that explains Waterloo. Let Christ's church work in harmony with the principles of righteousness laid down by Jesus, let her know nothing but to obey, and affrighted demons will come out of men and women on every side, for the church will be in league with Almighty God.

The expulsion of this demon was complete. He came out of the man that very instant. It is a great lesson, a lesson for a church never to forget, and a lesson for the state also. I have heard some men in public life say that some evils are necessary in the state. There is not on the earth one evil that is necessary.

Jesus had power to cast out demons then and he has the same power now. That fact should bring hope and joy to every one who is possessed by the demons of drink or lust or drugs or jealousy or covetousness or rebelliousness against God. Surely it is good news to them that there is One who can break the spell of such demons and drive them out and send them back to the pit whence they came. His name is Jesus. He is able to save unto the uttermost. That was why he came. He sets men free from the power of evil. He forgives, he cleanses, he saves, he gives new power to overcome evil with good. And he is the only one who can do these things for us and in us. He says, "Come unto me . . . and ye shall find rest unto your souls." He will not turn you away if you come to him with simple faith and trust like that of a little child. In his name I invite you to trust him, accept him and confess him even now as your Saviour and Lord. Come, yielding yourself to him as your rightful Lord and Master. Come now!

CHAPTER VII

Almost is Not Enough

Almost is Not Enough ✓

~~~~~~

> *Thou art not far from the kingdom of God.*
>
> —MARK 12:34

To REFRESH your memory, I read some verses from chapter twelve of Mark's Gospel:

> *And one of the scribes came, and having heard them reasoning together, and perceiving that he had answered them well, asked him, Which is the first commandment of all?*
>
> *And Jesus answered him, The first of all the commandments is, Hear, O Israel; The Lord our God is one Lord:*
>
> *And thou shalt love the Lord thy God with all thy heart, and with all thy soul, and with all thy mind, and with all thy strength: this is the first commandment.*
>
> *And the second is like, namely this, Thou shalt love thy neighbor as thyself. There is none other commandment greater than these.*
>
> *And the scribe said unto him, Well, Master, thou hast said the truth: for there is one God; and there is none other but he.*
>
> *And to love him with all the heart, and with all the understanding, and with all the soul, and with all the strength, and to love his neighbor as himself, is more than all whole burnt offerings and sacrifices.*
>
> *And when Jesus saw that he answered discreetly, he said unto him, Thou art not far from the kingdom of God.*

These verses point out four things for us: A lawyer's honest question, the positive answer of Jesus, the lawyer's discreet comment, and a solemn observation by Jesus.

A certain man, called a scribe by Mark and a lawyer by Matthew, heard the brilliant and silencing answers which Jesus made to captious and tricky questions asked him by three groups of his enemies, the Pharisees, the Herodians and the Sadducees. This lawyer was profoundly impressed by Jesus and the cleverness and wisdom of his replies that silenced and routed his enemies. Therefore the lawyer decided to ask Jesus an honest, serious and vital question. That question was, "Which is the first commandment of all?"

I believe that we are thoroughly justified in thinking that this lawyer did not ask his question captiously or insincerely or in a smart-aleck fashion. If he had asked his question in any such spirit as that, I am sure that Jesus would not have said to him, "Thou art not far from the kingdom of God." It is quite evident that this lawyer became sufficiently serious and earnest and honest, as he came face to face with Jesus, to justify Jesus in saying that he was near the kingdom of God. He must have realized that he was standing in the presence of one of great wisdom, one who spoke with a note of authority, one who possessed profound spiritual insight as to matters of religion. It was time for the lawyer to be deeply serious and to show his concern as to the most important of God's commandments.

I am emphasizing this lawyer's earnestness because it is so tremendously important that everyone should be thoroughly honest and serious and respectful when one's personal relations and obligations to God are under consideration. If we desire to know what are our highest duties unto God, what are his supreme commands unto us, then we dare not be superficial, shallow, flippant, or half-hearted in our quest for the truth. We must be whole-hearted; we must be reverent; we must be humble and earnest and honest.

82

This lawyer knew that there were many commandments of God. We would like to think that he believed they should all be kept. But he wanted to know which of God's commandments Jesus thought was the first, the greatest, the most important of all. The question he put to Jesus shows us two things. It shows us his interest in the laws, the commandments of God; and it shows us the high opinion he had already formed of Jesus. He seems to have had his own opinion as to which commandment was first of all, and he was pleased when the reply of Jesus confirmed his opinion on the subject.

Would that all lawyers were familiar with the laws of God and realized that his laws are the most important of all laws! One of the noblest of all callings is that of the lawyer. One of the finest opportunities any man has to bless his fellow man, to honor God, and to help stabilize society is the opportunity of the right kind of lawyer. If all lawyers believed that the first and second of all commandments of God are what Jesus said they are, then this would be a much better world.

Think of the lawyers in this church, this city, this nation of ours. Think of their influence, their power, their opportunities for good or evil. I rejoice that many of them are outstanding Christians. In fact some of the greatest lawyers of the long centuries have been great friends of Christ. That was true of Sir Thomas More, William Wilberforce, Sir William Blackstone, Simon Greenleaf, Charles Evans Hughes, and many others, perhaps less famous. And in passing, I wish to record my own deep sense of gratitude and affection for the large group of able and worthy lawyers who are members of our church here in Dallas. Often they cause my heart to rejoice by their Christian attitudes and behavior.

The Scripture basis for the message of this hour makes it clear that Jesus had respect for the integrity of the lawyer who questioned him about the first commandment of all.

An honest question deserves a definite answer. Jesus promptly gave that kind of answer to the questioning lawyer. He did not hesitate. He was definite, positive and scriptural in his reply. He quoted two declarations from the Pentateuch with which the lawyer was thoroughly familiar. The first was from Deuteronomy, chapter six, verses four and five: "Hear, O Israel; the Lord our God is one Lord: And thou shalt love the Lord thy God with all thy heart, and with all thy soul, and with all thy mind, and with all thy strength." The second was from Leviticus, chapter nineteen, verse eighteen: "Thou shalt love thy neighbor as thyself."

Matthew in reporting this incident quoted Jesus as saying to the lawyer, "On these two commandments the whole law hangeth, and the prophets." In other words, Jesus packed into his reply the very essence of both the law and the prophets. A man's relationship to God constitutes his highest responsibility. That is his supreme duty. The first and most important of all commandments deals with that duty of man. To love God supremely is to be rightly related to God. Anything less than that is a faulty relationship. It is no wonder that Jesus said that the first commandment of all is that one love God with all his heart, for out of the heart are the very issues of life. And Jesus knew that there could be no prospect of a man loving his neighbor as himself unless that man had first learned the secrets of love from God, who is love. Obedience to the first commandment is absolutely essential to the fulfillment of the second.

Thus Jesus sought to teach the basic truths of divine revelation to the lawyer, and, I am convinced, to us also. How teachable are we? The lawyer of our text was teachable to the extent that he gave verbal assent to the truth of the answer made by Jesus, as we can see from his discreet comment.

Note what he said: "Well, Master, thou hast said the truth: for there is one God; and there is none other but he: and to love him with all the heart, and with all the understanding, and with all the soul, and with all the strength, and to love his neighbor as himself, is more than all whole burnt offerings and sacrifices."

84

Yes, his was a discreet comment. Every Jew would readily agree that the statement, "The Lord our God is one Lord," was true. Many of them would agree that the first commandment as given by Jesus was also true. But when it came to the second commandment as stated by Jesus most of the Jews would have difficulty. They would be disposed to greatly limit the word "neighbor." They were not gifted in the divine art of loving their neighbors—the Samaritans, for example. This lawyer may have had some reservations in mind as to how far the word neighbor applied; but, even so, he admitted the truth of the idea in the second commandment.

In effect, what this man was saying in the presence of Jesus was something like this: "Undoubtedly the great matter of salvation is a matter of the heart, for to love God supremely is worth more than all whole burnt offerings and sacrifices. Salvation is not by forms. It is not by sacrifices. It is not by altars where beasts are laid as sacrifices and from which the smoke ascends. Salvation is a matter of the heart. Salvation is a matter internal, rather than external. The great thing is the question of the heart's proper relation to the Lord." Oh, but he was near the kingdom! How wonderfully near! No wonder is it that when Jesus saw how discreetly the lawyer made such comments, he said, "Thou art not far from the kingdom of God." In some respects this observation by Jesus was a compliment to the man and was intended as an encouragement to him. But it was also a faithful and solemn and surprising statement to the lawyer that he was not in the kingdom of God, although he was a strict Jew and had an objective knowledge of both the law and the prophets. He had come near the kingdom but had not entered into the kingdom. He had met the King but had not as yet accepted the King as his Lord and Saviour.

Oh, I am persuaded that I am speaking to some who are not far from the kingdom of God. You are serious, too, for God has dealt with you. You have crossed his path, and he has crossed yours. He has spoken to your deepest self. Long-

You have that ;

ings have been awakened within you, desires have been stimulated within you, anxiety has been aroused within you. The sense of duty has stood out before you clearly and majestically. The sense of need has been acute, as you remembered your weakness and frailty and moral loss. The sense of danger has sometimes filled you with fear. God has come near to you. And no doubt have I that the Master, as he searches your hearts, says to some of you, "Thou art not far from the kingdom of God."

And now I am coming to say the serious thing. You may come near the kingdom. You may come to the door of the kingdom. You may come close to the kingdom. And yet, in the last great, desperate, crisis hour you may turn away, you may fail, you may go backward, and not enter into the kingdom at all. Whether this lawyer entered in, the Bible does not say. One would fear from the after story that he did not. Though he was serious and candid and inquiring and had remarkable convictions about the soul's proper relations to God, one would fear, as he scans the narrative given by Matthew and Mark and Luke—all of them—that he came up and looked within, and then turned away from the beautiful gate. To be near the kingdom is not to be in it. To be near the kingdom does not mean that one will be saved. In this gospel land of ours, where men and women hear about Christ, I have not a doubt that many are near the kingdom but will not enter in. They come near, they see, they feel, they tremble, they desire, they resolve, they make great vows and high resolutions. But they do not make the great decision. They put that off to some more convenient season. They turn away, and they walk that same beaten, downward, worldly path they walked before.

To come near the kingdom does not mean that you will be in the kingdom. "Almost persuaded" is not enough. You remember what occurred when Paul stood before the ruler Agrippa and made his great defense of the Christian religion. When Paul finished his mighty testimony the trembling ruler there on his throne said to Paul, "Almost thou persuadest me to be a Christian." "Almost" is not enough. There is not any sign that Agrippa ever afterward took that matter up again. He said to Paul, "This will do now. I have heard all I can bear to hear now. You can go now. Almost thou persuadest me to be a Christian." Doubtless at that moment Agrippa was not far from the kingdom of God. He felt, he trembled, he quaked, he quivered, he confessed: "Almost do you persuade me to be a Christian"; but "almost" is not enough.

Five wise virgins filled their lamps with oil and went to the wedding feast. Five more failed to fill their lamps, and when they arrived and their lamps were not filled and their lights would not burn, they cried out in their pitiful plight, "Divide the oil with us. Help us." It was too late. "Open to us, open to us," they cried, but the door was shut. Opportunity comes once, opportunity tarries, opportunity beckons, opportunity appeals, opportunity mightily urges. Opportunity may be forfeited. One may come near, oh, so near, within a breath of getting into the kingdom of God, and yet turn away from that gate, and go the downward, deathward road forever.

Now, if one comes to the kingdom of God, let that one remember that he or she will not tarry long at that place—not long, not long! One's feelings do not remain at a certain level. One's feelings change; one's emotions change. A man in this city, whom I have seen sob like a child under the preaching of the gospel, said to me a while ago—he is a rich man now, "I would give one round million dollars if I could cry like I used to cry twenty years ago, when I heard you preach." He had come near. Feelings had been disturbed, emotions had been kindled, great fires of anxiety, of concern, of conviction, had burned within him, like a furnace. He had come near, but the fires died down. He did not act, he did not follow the light, he did not obey. But not long ago, with pathos inexpressibly in his voice, he said to me, "One round million dollars would I gladly give, if once again I could cry as I used to cry twenty years ago, when I heard you preach." There is not anything in the world more pitiful than that. There is not anything in the world more alarming than that. There is not anything in the world more distressing than that.

(2)
One may come near, but he will not stay near. He will enter into the kingdom of God, or he will go backward and downward, and farther and farther away. A human soul is like that. If one has a conviction and does not follow it, that conviction becomes weaker. If a man follows his conviction, he is stronger in it than ever before. When a man commits himself to any course of conduct, good or bad, he is stronger in that course after such commitment. When a man has a conviction and fails to follow it, he is weaker and his conviction is weaker. When a man has truth outlined before him, he sees it, he faces it, he feels it, his soul wants it, and then turns back and turns away, that truth gets dimmer and dimmer.   'ILLUS - DEN·O·M. -PROGRESS . PARTI/ TRU/

Man after man has said to me, "I began back yonder with profound reverence for the Bible and for the sayings of Jesus, but now I question it all." Of course he does. If a man faces truth and does not follow the truth, does not heed the truth, does not obey the truth, does not act upon the truth, that truth becomes dimmer, until at last he will question it all. A man's religious impressions are like blossoms on our fruit trees in the garden. The blossoms will soon turn into fruit, or the passing winds will blow those blossoms away. Such are man's religious impressions. One does not stay concerned about himself, anxious and burdened and filled with foreboding and apprehension. One does not stay in that temper very long. One goes on, one acts, one resolves, one chooses, one decides, one gives up, one yields; or one goes back and down and the impressions fade away. A bad habit in life fits us deeper into the groove, and deeper into the grave, for the words "groove" and "grave" come from the same root. One gets in a groove—he is getting into a grave. A man can have habit set against God, neglectful, forgetful, captious, disobedient, on into that groove he will go, until presently his groove will end in his grave.

O my brother men, my gentle women, my happy boys and girls, you can come near, you can be moved, you can be disturbed, you can be filled with concern, you can tremble, you can pray, you can say, "Oh, that I knew where to find Christ; oh, that I had my sins forgiven and were saved"; you can say that and feel that, and yet turn away and go downward, and miss the way of hope and light and salvation.

What is there for you to do? Just one thing. Make an honest surrender of yourself to Christ, because he is the Saviour, nor is there any other. He is the Saviour of the old man, thank God, if the old man will only surrender. He is the Saviour of the middle-aged man, the Saviour of the father, who has put off his return to God down to the afternoon of life; the Saviour of the mother, with her gray hairs and her grown children, and yet without God—Jesus is the Saviour for her, if she will surrender to Him. He is the Saviour of one who came hard by the gates of death with a wasting sickness, and yet in answer to the prayers of some who had audience with God and power with God, that one was brought back—some woman, some man—and he or she is on the blessed footstool of God's mercy and grace. There is forgiveness for you, there is salvation for you, brought back from that great distress, affliction, and peril—salvation for you, if you will surrender to Christ, if you will just give up to Christ.

Though your difficulties are many, Christ is able to help you. Though your doubts are grave, Christ will solve them and save you, if you will surrender to him. Though your regrets and mistakes are poignant and bitter, Christ is mighty to change and save. Though your failures, your regrettable chapters, your lapses, are dreadful, yet God's Word says, "This is a faithful saying, and worthy of all acceptation, that Christ came into the world to save sinners." Whatever your case, whatever your doubt and fear, whatever your loss and failure, whatever your yesterday, whatever your today, whatever the long tomorrow, Jesus will forgive and keep and save you, if you will surrender to Him. "Almost" is not enough! "Almost" is but to fail!

The scientists tell us in their analyses of the chemicals that enter into this mineral or that, or this thing in nature, or the other, that the copper that we see lacks just the tiniest shade of being gold; but something in the composition came short, and it was copper instead of gold. Oh, what a difference between copper and gold! One can come near to the kingdom of God, can be within sight, within sound, of the messages and light and hope of the blessed world, and yet miss it all, and sink down, and go the way of defeat and loss and failure forever.

They tell us that the great matter is to take the first step. I wonder if that statement ought not to be changed. Is not the great matter to take the last step? Here are men and women who have taken the first step, have written down in their hearts great purposes about what they meant to do with Christ. They have taken the first step. They have felt, they have trembled, they have prayed, they have wished, they have hoped, they have vowed, they have resolved. Oh, it is not the first step that is most important! It is the last step! Take it tonight. "Him that cometh to me I will in no wise cast out." "Your sins may be as scarlet, I will save you, if you will come to me. You may be an old man or an old woman. I will save you, if you will come, but you must come." Do you say, "I am ready, I am willing, I am decided this night to surrender to Christ, that in his own way Christ may save me; and from tonight, in his own way, Christ may guide me"?

> *"Almost persuaded" now to believe;*
> *"Almost persuaded" Christ to receive;*
> *Seems now some soul to say,*
> *"Go, Spirit, go Thy way,*
> *Some more convenient day*
> *On Thee I'll call."*

90

"Almost persuaded," come, come today;
"Almost persuaded," turn not away;
Jesus invites you here,
Angels are ling'ring near,
Prayers rise from hearts so dear,
O wond'rer come.

"Almost persuaded," harvest is past!
"Almost persuaded," doom comes at last!
"Almost" cannot avail;
"Almost" is but to fail!
Sad, sad, that bitter wail—
"Almost—but lost!"

O soul, take hold of that rope thrown to you, and say, "It shall not be simply "almost," but it shall be "altogether," tonight, my surrender to Christ.

CHAPTER VIII

A Test of Friendship

C H A P T E R   V I I I

A Test of Friendship

~~~~~~

*Ye are my friends, if ye do whatsoever
I command you.*

—John 15:14

ONE OF the most inspiring words in the lexicon
of language is the word friend. In most of us, it awakens tender and inspiring thoughts. One is rich if he has worthy and true friends, and conversely, one is poor if he be without worthy and true friends. An asset, therefore, in life is the matter of one's friends and friendships. It is a pungent word that the Bible enjoins upon us in this language: "Thine own friend and thy father's friend, forsake not." If someone comes along and gives clear proof that he was your father's friend, your heart goes out to him at once. Your father's friend you at once adopt for your friend also. An asset in life, measureless in moment, is this matter of one's friends.

Friendship, as you know, involves reciprocal relations. We hear the old saying, "It takes two to make a quarrel," and it also takes two to make a friendship. Reciprocal relations are involved, so it is not a one-sided affair; there are two parties involved in this matter of friendship.

The English people have an expressive saying like this: "He is my friend who grinds at my mill." Jesus applies this word "friend" to his own people, to his own true followers. Hear him in his Word: "Ye are my friends if ye do whatsoever I command you." The highest possible honor in earth or Heaven is to be called truly the friend of Jesus. Abraham was called "the friend of God." Oh what an appellation! You may recall that Lord Brook requested that this inscription be put on his gravestone: "Here lies the friend of Sir Philip Sidney." Others have had themselves characterized like this: "the friend of Milton," "the friend of Browning," "the friend of Shakespeare."

Some years ago we had a man running for the governorship of this state and speaking of a former governor who was still living, the widely famed Governor Hogg. This candidate said to a little group of us, "Governor Hogg is my friend and his influence put with mine will elect me, I think," and it did.

Jesus comes and takes this blessed term "friend" and says to us, "Ye are my friends, if ye do whatsoever I command you." The supreme question, therefore, for you and for me to face is, "Are we the friends of Christ?" That is the supreme question. Let us impress that question upon our minds, upon our deepest conscience, "Am I really and truly a friend of Christ?" He is the friend of all. His death was for all. Am I his friend?

Now there are certain tests whereby we may pass wisely on this question, "Am I really, truly the friend of Christ?" I make three vital tests. First of all, you are the friend of Christ if you are truly trusting in him as your personal Saviour. "Whosoever putteth his trust in the Lord shall be saved," and this is more than any mere intellectual assent to the historic person called Jesus Christ. Intelligent people, no matter what their religious affiliations or pretensions, or lack of pretensions —intelligent people are aware that there once lived on the earth a person called Christ, that he came into the world and was crucified, and thereafter wielded a marvelous influence on the world.

It is not enough to say, "I believe that Christ was crucified, buried and rose again." That is not enough. Do I accept him as my Saviour? Do I commit myself to him with definite unreserved commitment, yielding to him, that he may be my Saviour? The devils know that Jesus is the Son of God and they tremble. The devil trembled when he was in the presence of Jesus' mighty works. Jesus drove demons out of human beings and demons trembled before him and cried out to Jesus, "What have we to do with thee, Jesus, thou Son of God? Art thou come hither to torment us before the time?" The devil and his demons know that Jesus is the divine Son of God, but they are not saved.

Have you put your trust in Jesus as your personal Saviour, so that you can say with Paul, "I know whom I have believed, and an persuaded that he is able to keep that which I have committed unto him against that day"? Those of you who know Greek know that Paul used there the Greek word which means a bank. Christ is a great banker. Paul said, "I have made my deposit with him. The bank is not going to break. No trouble is going to come to the bank. I know in whom I have committed my soul's salvation and am persuaded that he is able to keep all that I have committed unto him, even myself. My trust is in the Lord." "Commit thy way unto the Lord: Trust also in him and he will bring it to pass," even your salvation. All that you need to have done for you, that adequate, atoning, divine Saviour will do for you, if you will trust him as your Saviour. Are you trusting Him as your Saviour?

> *Other refuge have I none—*
>   *Hangs my helpless soul on Thee:*
> *Leave, ah, leave me not alone,*
>   *Still support and comfort me!*

> *All my trust on Thee is stayed,*
>   *All my help from Thee I bring;*
> *Cover my defenseless head*
>   *With the shadow of Thy wing.*

Are you trusting alone in Christ as your Saviour?

> *On Christ the solid Rock I stand,*
>   *All other ground is sinking sand.*

97

But now there is another test. If you are really the friend of Christ, then you love him. Oh how great a matter is this matter of loving Christ! You will love him with all your heart. If you are really his friend, you will love him to the extent that you will yield yourself to him, without reserve, that he may be your Saviour; accepting him, bowing before him in your heart.

Man believes unto righteousness with the heart. Out of the heart are the issues of life. Do you love Christ? O that fairest one among ten thousand, do you love him? As you think of what he has done for you and for all humanity, does your heart stir with strange outgoing of love toward him and for him? For if you do not love him, you are not his friend. You are not his friend whatever your pretention and profession, if you do not love him with a great love.

How serious is the absence of love in human relations. The absence of love in marriage robs the marriage state of all of its absent in the responsible relation of marriage, how serious is the problem that confronts the man and woman thus bound together!

and again about the absence of love in home life. If love is beauty and sacredness. How it grieves the heart to hear again

If love be absent from a church, that church is virtually dead. "By this shall all men know that ye are my disciples, if ye have love one to another." "We know that we have passed from death unto life, because we love the brethren"—we love one another, we love God's people. Solemn was the indictment brought against the church at Ephesus: "O church at Ephesus, I know thy work, thy labor, and thy patience, and thy orthodoxy. I know thy hatred against heresy and the rest. I have somewhat against thee because thou hast left thy first love. Repent or I will leave you and take the candlestick out of its place." A loveless church is a Christless church.

Men and women in the church are members of a family, brothers and sisters, a family of God that should be marked by love, and should be overflowing with love so that the outside world will say, "Behold how those Christians love one another." The Son of God loves me and gave himself for me. Do I love him? "God commendeth his love toward us, in that while we were yet sinners, Christ died for us." He died for me; do I love him? Trusting, yielding, joyful, obedient love is a proof that we are friends of Christ.

But there is still another test. I have spoken of two. We are friends of Christ if we definitely trust Him as our Saviour. If we are the friends of Christ, we distinctly, consciously love him as our Lord and Master. But more, if we are true friends of Christ, then we will try to obey him; we desire to obey him. "Ye are my friends," says our text, "if ye do whatsoever I command you." Here now is a great climaxing test that keeps on saying to us, "Why call ye me Lord, Lord, and do not the things which I say?" If we love him we will keep his commandments. A Christian wants to obey Christ.

The first question of the newly born Christian is the one put by Paul as he walked the Damascus road, after his spiritual visitation with Jesus. The first question Paul asked was, "Lord, what wilt thou have me to do?" The Christian wants to know what Christ wants done. The indifferent, inactive, disobedient Christian has an alarming suggestion that he might be mistaken in the character of his feelings toward Christ. "If ye love me, ye will keep my commandments."

Though our behavior may be marred and imperfect, yet if our eyes and hearts are in the direction of obeying according to the expressed will and word of Christ, then we are his friends. This test probes deep. It goes deeper than profession, yes, deeper than performance. Like the Word of God it is sharper than a two-edged sword, it pierces to the realm of the spirit and discerns the thoughts and intents of the heart. How

99

glad we should be that our Master can read our minds and knows what is in our hearts.

In the twenty-fifth chapter of Matthew we find a scene of the final judgment. As men are gathered before Christ in that day, we hear him say to those who had been kind to the poor and needy, "Inasmuch as ye have done it unto one of the least of these, ye have done it unto me." And to those who had not been kind to the poor and needy, he said, "Inasmuch as ye did it not unto one of the least of these, ye did it not unto me." There you see the positive relation, and also the negative relation. "Ye are my friends if ye do whatsoever I command you," and the negative relation as well: "Ye are not my friends, if ye do not the things I command you."

It would be serious behavior on the part of a soldier if he obeyed certain commands of his superior officer and discarded the others, saying, "I do not like those; I will reject them." It would be serious behavior if the druggist, looking over the carefully prepared prescription of the capable physician, should say, "Here are some elements that I will discard. I will cast them aside. I will fix up the prescription in part like I want it." That would be serious behavior. And it is serious behavior for us to say to Christ, "I hesitate here; I delay here; I refuse here." "Ye are my friends, if ye do *whatsoever* I command you."

Now what is it that Christ wants from us? He wants our friendship. May he have yours? Are you a friend of Christ? Do you trust him as your Saviour and do you in your heart love him because of who he is, and what he is, and what he has done and is doing and proposes to do for you and for our needy world? Do you love him? And does your heart want to do whatever he bids you do? Is there prompt response of your heart in obedience to his command to go and to do his command as given you here in the Word of God?

100

10,387

Do you want to know what Christ would have you do and then strive to do his bidding? You have said that, if you are a Christian. Jesus wants your friendship; your friendship expressed in faith, in love, in affection, in obedience. Do you give him that friendship? That is the gift supreme Jesus wants from you.

I could bring no word, I think, at this Christmas time more vital than this. Oh, that word, "friend," that word "friend." Christmas is a time when one ought to look over his friendships and see that they are in repair. See that you cherish your friends in the right way. Do not allow your friendships to be marred or impaired in a season of "Peace on earth, and goodwill toward men." Everybody should carefully examine the status of his friendships at this glad season, and especially one's professed friendship for Christ. That neglected present ought to be sent. The delayed token ought to be looked after. The long delayed letter ought to be written. The long delayed religious visit should be made. The renewed vows of faith, love and obedience to Christ should be made joyfully and sincerely.

Far and above all these human relations, important as they are, vitally important as they are, is this great matter: Do you have real friendship toward Christ? Do you bow to him gladly as your Lord and Master? Do you turn away from every other thing in this universe and turn to him? Have you committed your life and the keeping of your soul to that divine helper? Have you?

Will somebody say, "I am in my heart a friend of Christ but I have not made it known"? Oh, but you should make it known. For the sake of others you should make it known, and for gratitude to Christ you should make it known, that down in your heart, you do love Christ and you do want to obey him. Come out into the open!

O secret friend of Christ, if one is listening to me now, come out into the open for him now. Will somebody here this

101

evening say, "I never did come out for him. I never did confess publicly my faith in Christ. I never did put my destiny in Christ's hands. I never did yield my heart, myself, my life to him, but I am ready to do so now"? He waits, graciously waits. He calls to you and reaches out his arms and greets you and welcomes you. "Whosoever will, let him take the water of life freely," and "Him that cometh unto me, I will in no wise cast out." "Today, if you hear his voice, harden not your heart." "Behold now is the accepted time. Now is the day of salvation."

Perhaps there is somebody who says, "I have already made the commitment, the great definite surrender, and I am already in some church somewhere else, but my residence is now in this community, and my church membership ought to be here, and tonight I gladly come out into the open to link my church membership with this body of Christ's believers, with this family of God. I take my place in the church." Do you come?

A glad-hearted welcome awaits you. Christ offers you his undying friendship if you will take him at his word and do his bidding. It is in his name that you are invited and urged to surrender fully unto the King of kings, the Lord of lords, the Saviour of the world, the Friend supreme.

CHAPTER IX

Why Did Jesus Go Away?

Why Did Jesus Go Away?

~~~~~~

> *Nevertheless, I tell you the truth; it is*
> *expedient for you that I go away, for*
> *if I go not away the Comforter will*
> *not come unto you, but if I depart I*
> *will send him unto you.*
> —JOHN 16:7

Y̲OU recognize our text as the language of Jesus.
It was spoken the night before the crucifixion. On that
memorable occasion Jesus instituted the supper which it to be
observed in his churches till he shall come again. On that
same occasion he delivered the marvelous discourse found in
several chapters of the Gospel of John, from one of which
chapters this text is taken.

Tenderly, tactfully, Jesus led up to the announcement that
is made in this text. "I am going away." This announcement
utterly baffled the disciples. Oh, how much he meant to those
disciples! For three years he had been their guide, their
teacher, their companion. They had turned to him even as
the rose turns to the sun for warmth and refreshment and for
all needed strength.

"Can he mean that he is actually leaving us?" they won-
dered. "Does he not mean that he is weary and worn and
must have rest? Is he not suggesting that we have so worked
him, that we have so engaged him, that we have so taxed him
that he must have cessation from it for a while, that his weariness must be relieved, that rest must be had?"

No. Jesus' meaning is unmistakable. "I am going away, not
because the world does not understand me, not because my
tasks are so utterly consuming my powers, not because I have

been so sadly mistreated in the world; I am going away, O my disciples, because it is best for you."

Now are the disciples baffled indeed. Now are they confounded beyond all measure. "He is going away, and going, so he declares, for our own good. How can it be expedient for us that he go away?"

A little company they were, without prestige or power, and they were to be sent into the midst of a crooked and perverse generation, as sheep in the midst of wolves. On every hand their work would be opposed. Their cause and calling would be unpopular. How could it be expedient for them that he go away? They did not understand.

I guess that every one has felt as those disciples felt. Oh, that Jesus could stay here with us! You have felt it; I have felt it. Why could not he stay here so that we could see him, so that we could touch his hand, so that those lips could speak to us? Who has not felt that? That is the sentiment expressed in the song we sang as children:

> *I think when I read that sweet story of old,*
> *When Jesus was here among men,*
> *How he called little children as lambs to his fold,*
> *I should like to have been with him then.*

These disciples, true to human experience, felt consternation at the thought that it could be for their profit that he go away. "Nevertheless, I tell you the truth: it is expedient for you that I go away."

Surely, surely there were some great reasons for his going away, or Jesus would not have gone at all. Such reasons there are. Let us glance at some of them.

In this same farewell discourse Jesus had given them one great reason why it was needful for them that he go away. "I go to prepare a place for yu. And if I go and prepare a place for you I will come again and receive you unto myself, that where I am ye may be also." How considerate ever is

106

Jesus of his people! "Better for you, O my disciples, better for you is it that I should go. Human life is brief. It will not be long before each one of you will leave this earthly scene of trouble and sorrow. Where will you go then? Your hearts should be comforted in the knowledge that I go to prepare a place for you. And when the time comes for you to go I will come and take you, that where I am ye may be also."

The going of Jesus from the earth back to the Father included the crucifixion and death on the cross which was to follow on the morrow. His going included his resurrection on the third day as he himself foretold and as the Scriptures corroborated. His going meant not only his crucifixion and resurrection, but his ascension back to the Father, as he led captivity captive. His going meant his enthronement at the right hand of God, where all honor and power and glory are eternally to be his. And his going meant, as he here tells us, the preparation of our home, our final habitation, our eternal place of residence.

"I am going on your account. I am going to prepare a place for you in the Father's house of many mansions." The glorious things being prepared for us are beyond our imagination, for we are told, "Eye hath not seen, ear hath not heard, neither have entered into the heart of man the things which God has prepared for them that love him." We should rejoice that Jesus went away when he did, because when our time to go arrives our home over there will be ready for us!

There were other good reasons for his going. It was expedient that he go away because his going away was meant to teach the superiority of the spiritual over the material, the superiority of the invisible over the visible. For three years the disciples had been in his company. With one word from his lips and a touch of his hand they had seen the sick healed, the storms hushed, and the winds abated. And at his voice even death was restored to life. Those disciples, for awhile, thought that the mighty works and teachings of Jesus were dependent upon his physical presence in the world. But in time they found out that such was not the case. They learned that faith was more than sight; and that the spiritual is more powerful than the physical.

What if Jesus were here in the flesh today? His fame has gone out to the ends of the earth, and if he were here in the flesh today every ship from every land, every train from every quarter, every conveyance that men use for travel would be employed to bring the people of the world into his presence. If he were in the flesh in Palestine, where he spent his earthly days, and men knew he was there even as he was once there, every possible means of transportation would be used to take men to that land in order that they might approach Jesus. Do you not see that the spiritual, invisible Saviour is far more blessed and helpful and important than a material, visible Saviour? It is much better than if Jesus in the flesh were here or there or elsewhere on earth, and the people of earth in one uncounted multitude stood for miles about him. How impracticable it would be with that great striving to get to him!

It is no wonder, then, what Jesus said to his disciples. In effect he said, "It is expedient for you that I go away, for when I am gone I will send you One whom you cannot see with your eyes, but whom you can feel and communicate with and approach just as if you heard me and touched my hand."

A spiritual religion is the world's infinite need. "God is a Spirit, and those who worship him must worship him in spirit and truth." Now that Jesus has returned to the Father any man or woman or child in Dallas, in Jerusalem, in New York, in Africa, anywhere, at the same moment may approach him. That mother whose child is burning with fever has a Friend nearer to her than a mother—Jesus, the great spiritual Saviour. That sufferer in some dark room, so near the gates of death that the nurses and physicians will allow no rude feet to be heard in that chamber may say, "Saviour, art thou near?" And the answer comes, "I will never leave thee. Lo

108

I am with thee always even unto the end of the world." A spiritual Saviour man must have.

Jesus' going away meant also that faith is incomparably more important and blessed than sight. The lesson for us to learn in this connection is that we are to walk by faith and not by sight. The highest experience of the human life is to trust God, to lean on his word though the earth trembles, though the heavens are confounded, and though the firmament may be melted. The highest experience is to take God at his word. If Jesus were here where men could see him, grasp his hand, hear his voice, they would walk by sight and not by faith.

Faith is incomparably more important than sight. Here is man's never-ceasing temptation — to walk by sight, his never-ceasing propensity. That is the foundation and the meaning of ritualism in the church. In some places of worship images of all kinds are means that people use, seeking to put their faith in concrete expression. No image of any saint should be in any place of worship. The very core of ritualism is the tendency of men to walk by sight and not to take God at his word and walk by faith. "God is a Spirit and they that worship him must worship him in spirit and in truth." Oh, the pleadings of men to *see* things! How like Thomas we are when he said, "I will not believe what you tell me unless I see the print of the nails in his hands and unless I thrust my hand into his wounded side." How like Thomas we are! How much better it would be if Peter's statement were true of us: "whom having not seen, ye love; in whom, though now ye see him not, yet believing ye rejoice with joy unspeakable and full of glory."

The miracle of Christianity today is that millions love Jesus whom they never saw. "Whom having not seen, they love!" If I should put to you this question, "Did you ever see Jesus?" you would answer, "Certainly not." But if I asked this great audience, "Do you love him?" hundreds would answer, "Yes, better than I love father or mother or child do I love him."

That is the miracle and glory of the Christian religion. "Whom, having not seen, we love!"

Why did Jesus need to go away? One reason is that Jesus needed to go away in order to bring himself nearer to us. That seems paradoxical. Yet the truth is at hand in our own lives and is confirmed constantly in our own experiences. I know because so often I am called to stand in the midst of mourners as they put away their beloved dead. What eulogies I hear! How much the mother thinks of her child! Death emphasizes her joy in that child. The husband as he waits beside the casket of his wife who through the years had been his companion and helpmeet realizes, now that the brave heart has ceased its beating and the lips are still, how much she did mean to him. Her very going has emphasized her unspeakable preciousness. What eulogies, what panegryrics of praise are heard when our dead are put away from our sight! The departure of Jesus was intended to bring him nearer to us.

A great and godly minister, long-time pastor of the Church of the Strangers, tells of the death of his two-year old child. Far was he from his home in New York when the message came. Not much had he seen of the little fellow, he had been so busy. Not often had he been able to play with the child, his time was so consumed in his important work. Yet on that long ride home, at every turn of the car wheels, the love which he bore grew stronger and stronger. Speaking of this loss twenty-five years later he said, "My baby is as dear now as on that awful day when I came and looked on his white face. There never comes into my study a father whose voice is charged with sorrow as he tells me of his dead but that my child takes me by the hand and helps me as I conduct the funeral of that man's child.

The world did not understand Jesus when he was here in the flesh. They said he was a man in league with Beelzebub. People reproached him and put upon him contumely without measure. But now millions bow before him—kings, queens, parliaments, and great men and humble men alike cry out, "We have found him whom our souls love." His going brought him nearer to us. Jesus is closer to us today than when he came from Joseph's new tomb; closer because he went from us.

Why did Jesus go away? The text tells us one other great reason. I have reserved that for the last. The Comforter—"I will send him unto you," the Comforter who is the Holy Spirit. Oh, this doctrine of the Holy Spirit is exceedingly simple if we but see the truth. The Holy Spirit does not come to witness for himself. Never a word has he for himself. He comforts us with Christ's wonderful words and the still more wonderful deed, even Christ's atoning death on Calvary. The Holy Spirit takes the truth which is in Christ Jesus, and makes it available to every man, the man in New York, in Calcutta, in Africa, in Dallas.

Concerning the Holy Spirit Jesus said, "When he is come he will reprove the world of sin and of righteousness and of judgment; of sin because they believe not on me; of righteousness because I go to my Father, and ye see me no more; of judgment, because the prince of this world is judged."

How will that moral man know that he needs Christ if the Holy Spirit convict him not of sin? How will he understand that he must be born again? How will he see it unless the Holy Spirit convict him of sin?

To his disciples Jesus said, "When I am gone the Spirit of Truth will come and explain many things you cannot understand now. He will interpret my words and give them entrance into your hearts and you will understand."

I saw one in the last week utterly overwhelmed with a great grief, but in answer to prayer the heart was calmed. Whence that calmness? It was by the power of the Holy Spirit. Christ's friends are commissioned to perform mighty works—works

111

that are impossible without the induement of divine power. Let us thank God that such power is available. Who can doubt it? The Holy Spirit gives us the power for these great works. The church or the preacher who minimizes the work of the Holy Spirit will not have that power.

"Ye shall receive power after that the Holy Spirit is come upon you, and ye shall be witnesses unto me in Jerusalem, and in all Judea, and in Samaria, and unto the uttermost parts of the earth." And Jesus told how we can receive the power of the Holy Spirit: "If ye then, being evil, know how to give good gifts unto your children, how much more shall your heavenly Father give the Holy Spirit to them that ask him?"

What truths are we to learn from this saying of Jesus? I mention several. First, we learn that the possession of the Holy Spirit is a divine gift from our heavenly Father. Second, we learn that our heavenly Father is more able and ready to give us this best of gifts than any earthly father knows how to give good gifts to his children. Third, not only must we desire to have the blessings of the Holy Spirit bestowed upon us, but we must ask the heavenly Father for them. And surely all of us should earnestly desire those blessings; for when the Holy Spirit is given to us we receive comfort, illumination, inspiration and power. Under the influence of the Holy Spirit we are enabled to repent of our sins, to exercise saving faith in Jesus Christ the Saviour, we are born again, that is we are regenerated and given the power to become the children of God. The Holy Spirit takes the deep truths of God and shows them unto us.

Jesus would have no church nor preacher nor any other child of God ever ignore or minimize or forget the functions and power of the Holy Spirit, the third person of the blessed Trinity. When he said, "It is expedient for you that I go away," it meant that he was ushering in the age, the dispensation, the full functioning of the Holy Spirit among the children of men.

112

Well may we sing:

Come, Holy Spirit, heavenly Dove,
With all Thy quickening powers;
Kindle a flame of sacred love
In these cold hearts of ours.

Come, Holy Spirit, heavenly Dove,
With all Thy quickening powers;
Come, shed abroad a Saviour's love,
And that shall kindle ours.

CHAPTER X

Obedient Witnesses

CHAPTER X

Obedient Witnesses

~~~~~~

> *But the angel of the Lord by night
> opened the prison doors, and brought
> them forth, and said: 'Go, stand and
> speak in the Temple to the people all
> the words of this life.'*
> —ACTS 5:19, 20

W E ARE to think together this morning for a little
while on Christ's method for Christian work. Our text is from
the fifth chapter of the book of Acts, nineteenth and twentieth
verses: "But the angel of the Lord by night opened the prison
doors, and brought them forth and said: 'Go, stand and speak
in the Temple to the people all the words of this life.' " The
text directs our attention to the second persecution of the
early church.

The progress made by the early church in its witness and
work for Christ was one of the wonders of all Christian history. A little company without prestige or prominence or
power began to witness for Christ and preach Christ; and in
a generation the pagan empire of Rome felt the impact of the
Christian message. Such success on the part of the early
church called forth vigorous persecution by the Sadducees.
This was an aggressive sect of the Jews during the time of
Christ's ministry. Their successors are with us yet. The
Sadducees were materialists. They did not believe in the
resurrection nor in angels. Man came from the earth and
would return to the earth, was their belief.

Now the teaching of the apostles concerning the resurrection of Jesus caused a mighty awakening among the people,
and the Sadducees, the materialists of that day who did not

believe in things spiritual, sought to stamp out this new religion which was spreading so fast among the people. The way of persecution is always a failure. It may seem to succeed but it does not succeed. The blood of the martyrs became the seed of the church. In spite of persecutions the disciples were bold, and the number of believers multiplied. The eternal purposes of God can not be defeated by men. Persecution can never win.

There are persecutions abroad now in the earth. These persecutors of Christianity are foredoomed to defeat because of God. Satan can never dethrone God. These Sadducees sought to blot out Christianity by persecution, so they took the apostles and put them all in jail and said, "Guard these men. Let none escape."

They silenced the preachers, did they not? No! An angel of the Lord came in the night, opened the prison doors, took all the apostles out and gave them the charge, "Go to the Temple and teach there to the people all the words of this life." And they did as the angel bade them. When morning came it was discovered that the prisoners were gone, to the utter confusion of the Sadducees. So they said, "Whereunto will this grow? We are confronted with something which forebodes distress for us, whereunto will it grow?"

While they were pondering what steps to take, one came saying, "We went to the prison and the doors were shut and the keepers were all there on guard but all the prisoners were gone and we found them in the Temple, preaching Christ to the people!" Officers were sent who arrested them and they were arraigned before the authorities. Sharp words were said to them by those overpowering, persecuting men. Simon Peter spoke first saying, "We ought to obey God rather than men. The officers told us not to preach any more in his name, but the angel of the Lord who brought us out of the prison said, "Go, stand and speak in the Temple to the people all the words of life. We ought to obey God rather than men."

And you know the rest of the story. They were beaten and bruised and then turned loose and threatened and warned not to preach any more. But they went right on with their teaching and preaching.

There are vital truths for us in this incident. Christ's messengers are here indicated, and the message which they are to give is here announced. An angel delivered the apostles from prison and told them, "Go, stand and speak in the Temple to the people all the words of this life." Angels were not to be preachers, men were to be the preachers. Angels are not preachers now; they are bright spirits, unfallen, holy, sinless.

One wonders, "Would an angel not make a great preacher?" No, he would be too far away from us. We must have someone "touched with the feeling of our infirmities." He was "tempted in all points like as we are, yet without sin," that he might be a Redeemer, a Saviour of lost men. He took our place under the law of God and took all our chastisement, all in his own body on the cross for us. An angel cannot be the preacher.

You and I will have to be the witnesses for Christ, poor as we are. When you think of it, what an honor this is to man that the Lord would make us his fellow workers, "workers together with him," to declare his own truth. What an honor to man! And how much better it is for a man to do this rather than for a ministering spirit who never knew what sin was, never tasted its bitter dregs, had no conception of the battles and misery through which sin plunges us mortals. An angel could not qualify. That is the work for redeemed men and women. What an honor to man and what a blow it is to Satan!

You will recall how David the stripling slew Goliath the giant with a stone from a sling which David hurled in the name and power of God. Goliath the giant scorned David the lad. God ever intends that the giants of evil be slain by

119

the word of truth proclaimed by his faithful preachers, even though they are merely human beings.

Long years ago King Edward's son, the Black Prince, was fighting fiercely at a battle front. The battle was going against him and word came to the King: "Your son is in a serious place. You had better send him reinforcements." But the King said, "No. Let him face it." And face it he did, and he won the battle. Oh, what honor it brings to our Lord when we stand for Christ, when we hold aloft the banner of the cross.

Men and women redeemed by the Lord Christ are to be witnesses; not angels, but men and women such as we are. Oh, what must the angels in heaven think of us? If they could speak to us, do you imagine they would say, "O men and women, why do you spend your time in vanity and leisure? Why do you waste your minds and your hearts on things that perish? Why are you so engrossed by the things that are just for to-day? Why not put your emphasis continually and supremely on the things of eternal moment?"

Men and women saved by Christ, we must carry the news of salvation to a lost world. We must tell them in Dallas and in Texas and in America, and in Europe, Asia, and Africa, and around the globe, about Christ. Redeemed men and women must do this, not angels.

The angels came and took these men out of prison and said, "Go, stand and speak in the Temple to the people, all the words of this life. Go to the Temple where the Sadducees are, where the people gather. Go where they come in great numbers, and there speak to the people all the words of this life. It is night but go to the Temple without delay. The King's business requireth haste. Get you on your mission."

Christ and Christianity know nothing about the line of demarcation between classes. Christ's gospel is to pioneer all popular education and all liberty and all real abiding progress. It does not know anything about preaching one gospel to the rich and another to the poor. All are needy sinners alike in the sight of God. "Go and speak to all the people!"

That was a bad day back yonder when a line was drawn and on one side they placed the laity and on the other side they placed the clergy. The clergy functioned and the laity looked on and stayed far off and nothing came of it but strife, which added to the darkness of the Middle Ages. That is not Christ's plan. If a layman can speak of Christ, then he must; then he sins if he does not. The Bible knows nothing about the distinction between the clergy and the laity. Every man and woman who can witness for Christ must do so. That is God's plan. Many times a layman can give a powerful witness in his place of business, a witness for Christ of eternal moment.

The Bible tells of many active laymen. Abraham was a layman, and Isaac and Jacob were laymen. Caleb and Joshua were laymen, Nehemiah was a layman, the three Hebrews cast into the fiery furnace were laymen. Philip and Stephen were laymen. The Bible magnifies laymen. Oh, the blight, the darkness, that settles down upon the land if laymen and laywomen imagine they have measured up to the full measure of their duty, their responsibility, when they come to the church on Sunday and give their little mite and go away and forget all about it in everyday life. They are in the world to represent Christ. But they misrepresent him by such conduct.

Now what about our message? These men were arraigned before their enemies and were persecuted and beaten. What about their message? The word spoken by Peter to the officers is the right word for Christians to speak today: "We ought to obey God rather than men." That is the foundation for us, that is an immovable stone. "We ought to obey God rather than men." We ought to obey God if it gets us in jail. That is the spirit the world needs now. The world is in chaos when it does not obey God. If all men obeyed God we would have peace to the ends of the earth.

The lust for gain, the lust for power, the lust for prominence, the lust for position, everywhere, is the thing that lures men downward in their way. "We ought to obey God rather than men." That is a great teaching, the sovereignty of God. All men must answer to God. The will of God, the law of God, is God's program for humanity.

Oh, for men to have the well-defined conviction that the will of God is to be followed whatever it may cost! Oh that the will of God could be done, from one end of this land to the other! If we coud hear our statesmen call the people back to God as did George Washington as he said, "If we ignore God and disregard his precepts, the nation is on the downward way." If we could have that kind of call, we would have more hope for our nation. America, like other nations, is headed for disaster if she disregards the will of God. We have a great heritage. We have a great background. We have had marvelous forebears. But if we disobey the will of God, play fast and loose with morality, with the high standards of truth and integrity and righteousness, we are headed straight for overwhelming defeat and perdition. "We ought to obey God rather than men."

There it is. That is our message laid out for us. We are to obey the Lord Jesus Christ. Our gospel is the gospel of a person. It goes beyond all organizations and forms and ceremonies and goes straight to him. Here is one who died for us and we put our case in his keeping. We yield to him. We are turned by his help from every evil way, and trustfully, submissively follow him and his way. Salvation is by Christ. These apostles said, "We have tried him; we have experienced him; we have tested his gospel in our lives. We are not preaching to you a fable. We are preaching to you the facts which we have personally tested and experienced." And that is my sermon today. Will you make this message personal in your lives? There are enough men and women in this great auditorium today, together with the greater radio audiences now hearing this simple discourse, who, if they would witness and work for Christ would cause wonders unceasing to follow in the wake of such witness and work.

When did you talk to someone about Christ? When did you, lawyer, a Christian man, talk to your fellow lawyer; or you, physician, to your patient, or the merchant to his friend? Oh, my soul, to think of a Christian living for months and maybe years, or even for days, without having a talk with somebody, quietly and seriously about his or her personal relation to the Lord! Are you silent on that great matter when you are left in the world specifically and preeminently for that purpose? There are enough here to do great things in just a short time if we would witness for Christ. We are not to loiter on the road. Do you say, "I have waited; I have been indifferent, inactive"? Oh, with a great resolve say, "I today am going to try from this day forward to please God, to be a witness for him."

Are there those here today who say, "I never came out for Christ, but down in my heart I now say 'Yes' to him"? Come out for him openly. "Ye are my friends if ye *do* whatsoever I have commanded you." Do you say, "I have waited. I have postponed"? Have you not waited long enough and is not his mercy sufficient motive for you to come today?

> *Oh happy day that fixed my choice,*
> *On Thee, my Saviour and my God.*

Who says, "I am for Christ and want to be with his people; I have already taken him as my Saviour; I am already a member of the church yonder, where I came from but now I live in Dallas and want to unite with this church"? We want you and with heart and hand and whole soul we say, "Come and thrice welcome."

Who says, "I have never accepted Christ as my Saviour but I have thought about it and pondered over it, and now in this great hour, this hour of destiny, I make my commitment"? Come now and link your life openly with Christ and his blessed church.

CHAPTER XI

A Basic Principle of Life

C H A P T E R   X I

A Basic Principle of Life

~~~~~~

It is required in stewards, that a man
be found faithful.

—I Cor. 4:2

IF OUR LIVES are to be lived wisely and worthily they must be undergirded by wise and worthy principles. The highest and chiefest principle of life is the principle of stewardship. This is the great regulative principle of life, the principle of stewardship of every talent and asset and resource that we have, the stewardship of life itself.

Paul stated it for us in this often quoted sentence: "It is required in stewards that a man be found faithful." The true meaning and mission of life are set out pointedly and comprehensively in this little word "steward." "It is required in stewards that a man be found faithful." Who and what is a steward? He is not an owner nor a proprietor, but he is one who has been entrusted with the affairs of another. From beginning to end, the Bible magnifies the principle of stewardship in its large reach and application. One thinks of Eliezer, the faithful steward in the house of Abraham, and one thinks of Joseph, the faithful steward in the house of Potiphar. You will recall in the account of his relations to Potiphar that the Bible tells us that Potiphar left all, everything pertaining to his house, in the hands of his steward "and he knew not ought he had, save the bread which he did eat," which was provided for him. Here then stands out the true meaning and mission of life—it is stewardship.

Paul states the principle for us in the great word "debtor." "I am debtor," said Paul, "both to the Greeks, and to the

Barbarians; both to the wise, and to the unwise," the people of his race and of every other race. Paul felt that he was debtor to the people of his land and of every other land. "I am debtor to humanity. I owe myself to humanity. I am obligated to humanity." Paul put it in that great way.

Jesus stated it for us in many statements. One of the most impressive being: "I came not to be ministered unto, but to give my life a ransom for many." Then this mission he gave us: "As my Father hath sent me into the world, even so send I you." We are to walk in his steps, to incarnate his Spirit, to carry out in our day and generation the mission he gave us.

More than a century ago the doctrine that was often accentuated in various sections of the world was the doctrine of "men's rights." Much literature at that time was permeated by that doctrine. The French Revolution was an attempt to regenerate society on the purely secular doctrine of "men's rights." It cannot be done with that doctrine. But if there should be set over against it, the Christian doctrine of men's duty, of their obligations, we begin to see clearly the true mission of life.

Jesus marked faithfulness as the highest criterion of character. He set out faithfulness as the supreme test of life. Paul's word is worthy of our earnest meditation today and all the days, namely: "It is required in stewards that a man be found faithful." Great thoughts emerge from this simple, but very far reaching statement. We have time for meditation briefly on two or three of these thoughts today.

First of all, our stewardship must be accounted for. Mark that imperious word, "must." There is no evasion, no neutral course possible. Everyone must give an account of himself to God. We must have our reckoning with him, for the use or abuse of life's privileges, life's trusteeship. This doctrine is the great regulative principle of life. If we build our lives on petty rules and ignore this great doctrine of stewardship, then we have lost one of the greatest privileges of life. All that we have and are and can be belong to God, and our use of these things constitutes our stewardship. We must render our account for this stewardship.

One can well understand how Daniel Webster would say that the most solemnizing thought that ever coursed through his mind and heart was the thought of his individual responsibility. Chief Justice Taft, a little before he went away into the great Beyond, in one of his noblest utterances said, "There is a lack of a realization of the sense of personal responsibility in this country which bodes no good for our civilization, but which breeds evil if we allow that relaxed sense of personal responsibility to go on unchanged." All stewardship, whatever it is, must be accounted for. Now we are prone to think that in our little ordinary lives it amounts to little. We can think of great personalities that sweep through the world; and we say certainly they will have a great stewardship to answer for. We can think of Napoleon marching across great nations carrying terror and horror for the people in the path of his awful march. We can think of men since his time, and of men now in the world, whose behavior seems to demand vast accountability by and by; but we are to remember that in our ordinary, everyday lives, we are just as directly responsible to God as is the mightiest personality who ever ruled or reigned.

Thackery, a noble worker for humanity, tells us that he was most of all influenced in his life by a very humble servant woman. Her spirit was so glorious that it radiated a constant challenge and inspiration to all who came within the radius of her humble life. Henry Ward Beecher, one of America's greatest orators, tells us that the most influential factor in his life, outside of his own father's family, was a plain Negro man, Cyrus Smith, whose Christian spirit was so humble and worthy that every time he came anywhere within the radius of that humble Negro's life, he was challenged to higher and better living. One of the most artistic and worthy tributes paid by Beecher to anybody in all the great orator's lifetime was paid by him to this humble servant. You and I, in our small spheres, are accountable to God as verily as Washington or Gladstone, or the greatest, mightiest or most famous on earth.

We must all give an account to God for the use or abuse of our time. Men sometimes speak of killing time. Oh, what a terrible onslaught they are making when they are killing time. What do you do with your leisure hour? With libraries accessible, with great sources of information, with night schools, with all kinds and forms of self-improvement knocking at your door, what do you do with life's leisure hour? How terrible to kill time, to waste time, the stuff of which life is made. We will answer for the use or abuse we make of our time. We will answer for all of life's talents, whatever they may be, though they are widely different in various lives, we still answer for them, every one.

Jesus spoke a parable of talents to the people. Five talents were given to one man, two talents given to another, and one talent to another. "Take ye and trade with them and make your report to me by and by," said the Master. And after a while the man with five talents came back and said, "Here Master, your five talents have made five more; here are ten talents." "Well done, good and faithful servant, thou hast been faithful over a few things. I will make thee ruler over many things." The two-talented man came back and said, "Here are your two talents. I have doubled them and made four." And he received exactly the same reward as was given the five talent man. The one talent man came and said. "I was afraid and I hid your talent in the earth; here it is." And the talent was taken away from him and given to the man who had ten talents. He forfeited it; lost it, by his unfaithfulness.

Now, in the parable of the talents and also in the parable of the pounds, and in all of the teachings of Christ, the truth is witnessed vividly as though it were written across the skies in letters of living fire, that our every talent must be accounted for. Our lives will be magnified, dignified and glorified if we lay faithfully to heart this vital truth.

The strong must bear the burdens of the weak. The educated must be patient with the untaught and the uneducated. The man of knowledge has the advantage over the man who does not have knowledge. The secure foundation of the state is laid, not in ignorance, but in knowledge. What a responsibility upon the educated man, upon the man who grapples with great groups of people, upon the man who speaks to vast audiences with the purpose of informing and influencing them. The educated man! What a responsibility he has! What a responsibility rulers have. "When the righteous are in authority, the people rejoice; but when the wicked beareth rule, the people mourn." The people, to an awful degree, take their cue from those in authority, and if those in authority lower the standards and allow the banners to droop, all the people will feel the blight and hurt following in the wake of such misbehavior.

Our talents, whatever they may be, are a trusteeship for which we must give our account by and by, and directly to God. We must every one render unto him an account for the deeds done in the body. Whatever our talents are, this or that or the other, mark it well, and never forget it, we must answer for our trusteeship.

Take the trusteeship of trial, suffering, pain and tears. That is a very real trusteeship. In recent hours I have talked to some passing through deep vales of suffering and trial and that question has leaped to their lips and pressed down upon their hearts. "Why this, when all my plans were being formulated upward and onward beyond anything in the past?" Sufferings and trials, pain and fears, these are all a part of the trusteeship of life. Hezekiah said, when he got through with his trials and looked back upon them and saw how he had been uplifted and fortified through them: "By these things men live." Milton put it thus: "Who best can suffer, best can do." Let us remember that testing days come to all, to the

131

righteous as well as to the wicked. Blessed is the man who measures up during the testing times.

When we are in the fiery furnace or in the lion's den, when affliction enthralls us, when disappointments confront and seek to dismay us, let us remember that our behavior through such trying days must be for human good all around us and for the glory of God. The whole world is better for the story of the high behavior of Job, that patriarch in the land of Uz. His property was swept from him in one stroke and all his children were carried into death in one day; his own health failed; his erstwhile friends deserted him, and even his own wife said, "Husband, curse God and die." You recall his reply: "Let come on me what will, though he slay me, yet will I trust in him." Millions and millions have read that story, and been fortified by it. They have been reassured by the high behavior of that grand old man who passed through suffering, perhaps as none other of all the children of men.

Whatever your trial, behave through it bravely. "For our light affliction is but for a moment." God will work out our affliction for the best for us. We must remember that the eyes of the world around us are focused on us. The eyes of young people and neighbors are turned upon us in the dark and cloudy day. How we need to bear up under that!

If I may be personal for a moment, I well remember when a great sorrow enthralled me and I could not see the way out for days. I remember a cruel penman put it on paper: "We will see how the minister's philosophy can bear a thing like this through which he is passing." But the day came on apace, when deliverance and mercy came from God and the clouds went away. The mists lifted and brightness and blessedness came. Let us be careful how we behave in the dark and cloudy day.

We should realize our responsibility for our influence. Our influence is indestructible. The influence of what we say or what we do, be it good or bad, abides to bless or curse. When a stone is dropped into a placid pool, the wavelets reach to the outer banks of that pool. It is that way with influence. It reaches to the shores of eternity, for good or evil. "No man liveth unto himself and no man dieth unto himself." His influence goes on and on. Those men who have stained the centuries with their destructive power must reckon with all the accumulation of miserable influences resulting from their bad behavior.

That marvelous genius, Napoleon, quoted: "Man proposes and God disposes," but he added cynically: "I propose and I dispose," and brushed aside with his hand the thought of God's Providence. But you remember when he made his fearful invasion into Russia that the storms and snow and physical conditions were so terrific that his loss of men was appalling and his defeat inevitable. He came back with head down, somewhat subdued and said, "God Almighty has been too much for me." And he is too much for any man who dares try to change God's plans. Victor Hugo said, as only Victor Hugo could say it, "This Napoleon bothered God." But men will not bother him forever. God calls the mighty to account as well as the humble. All are trustees and must render an account of their stewardship.

Oh, what a trusteeship is parenthood! Every time our Lord gives a little babe into the parents' keeping, he gives the commission: "Take this child and rear it for me." If we fail at that vital point, someday we may stand like David in the gate with utterly broken hearts and will wail out our cry, "O my son, Absalom, my son, my son, Absalom! would God I had died for thee, O Absalom my son, my son!" Let our trusteeship as parents be without reproach!

We may not, must not, dare not, ignore our vital trusteeship as citizens. If there are bad conditions in the social order, you and I are responsible. If we have officers who are unworthy in any realm, high or low, whose fault is it? They did

133

not elect themselves; they did not promote themselves. The votes of the people put them in their places. Let us mark well our behavior there. "When the righteous are in authority the people rejoice, but when the wicked beareth rule the people mourn." We put men in authority. Let us seek wisdom for the day when we are to choose our leaders and officers for church and for state.

Then there is the trusteeship, not only of influence in the home life, political life, social life, governmental life, there is the deepest influence of all—in moral and religious life. How great is the Christian's responsibility in the matter of his example! Gladstone said, "One example is worth a thousand arguments." "Ye are the light of the earth, but if the salt have lost its savor, wherewith shall it be salted? It is henceforth good for nothing, but to be cast out and to be trodden under foot of men." Is your example a good witness for Christ?

And then I come to speak a word about our material property. We must answer to God for the use or abuse of every piece of material property that ever comes into our hands. Man's material property and possessions, money—this also is a part of his stewardship, his trusteeship. What should be said about this? Two or three things. First of all, let us see well to the methods whereby this property is acquired. This property is to be acquired righteously, and if it be not acquired righteously, then down the road somewhere, some shaggy prophet shall stand at the gate when we arrive there and say to us, "This which you have taken is not yours; you are a thief and a robber." Our hands will be burned and our consciences seared if we get this property by unrighteousness, by dishonesty by trickery. Therefore, it follows that every sort of short-cut, every scheme of gambling, enervates and injures. Let us be sure that we get our property honestly and righteously.

I was felicitating one of our men on certain gains he had made in the realm financial and his face brightened as he said,

"Pastor, every dollar of it is a clean dollar." It all *should* be clean. You can no more trifle with gambling and think you can come out unharmed, unhurt, than you can trifle with rattle-snakes and be unhurt. How we get our property and make our money are vital considerations.

When property is secured, let us understand all along, "This is a part of my God-given stewardship in the world. I am to give an account of it all. He has entrusted this to me. I must not trifle with it. I am a steward. I must make the right use of it, the fullest and best use of it." The man who does not have that understanding of property has missed the meaning of it.

All life's talents, privileges, assets and power are a part of our stewardship. "I am debtor to humanity," taught Paul, "and all that I have bound up with me, the money in my purse, all is a part of my debtorship. I owe my best for humanity." This is the high mission of life. Now, we are to remember how to get it and when we get it we are to remember that it is a trusteeship. We are to know that if we do not remember that our property is a trusteeship, then we will have the question asked, as by the ancient prophet Malachi, "Will a man rob God?" Why, is it possible for a man to rob God? It is. You can rob God just as certainly as you can rob a bank, a store, or a private home. You ask wherein have we robbed God, and the answer comes back—"In tithes and in offerings." You have withheld these. You have gone on living as though all this is yours, without any idea of trusteeship. You have forgotten God. Now, your gold and silver will be taken and your vines will wither and your fruit will decay if you trifle with God.

Then the prophet goes on to say: If you will, change your ways and

> *Bring ye, all the tithes into the storehouse, that there may be meat in mine house, and prove me now herewith, saith the Lord of hosts, if I*

135

will not open you the windows of heaven, and
pour you out a blessing, that there shall not be
room enough to receive it.

Oh, if humanity only realized as it ought the stewardship
of property, we would not have an orphan home begging, nor
a hospital bedraggled and failing, nor a great school with
inadequate equipment. Every great cause of education, of religion, and of benevolence would be undergirded and carried
forward, if men would play the game as they should play it
in the sight of God.

Let us be orthodox in this matter of stewardship of our
property. Let us be citizens of the kingdom of heaven, high
on the road of devotion and obedience in doing the will of
God. You ask, "How much shall I give?" Surely you would
not be willing to give less than the ancient Jew with his greatly
reduced light as compared with ours. He gave his tithe and
then came again with offerings. Shall we give less than the
Jews gave in the long ago? Certainly no Christian would
be willing to give less than the tithe, conscientiously, and reg-
ularly and in addition thereto, he will be moved again and
again to bring offerings of thanks, love offerings to great
causes.

Another word needs to be said about our property. A recent book tells the thrilling story of the lives of Mr. and Mrs.
John G. Hardin, a modest couple who rose early and toiled
late and accumulated their property. A little while before
they went away they gave nearly two millions to various institutions, orphanages, hospitals, and schools. Read that story
and you will find one note in it that our day and generation
needs to lay to heart. That ranchman out yonder on the
plains said, "I saved my property, not as a miser, but as a
steward, and my wife helped me to save it. We did not consciously waste a dollar of it on things that were unnecessary
in our lives."

You could make that money that you are ready to fling away on little nothings to blossom like Eden blossomed, if you invest it for God. Put it in a boy or a girl whom you send away to school. They will some day be citizens whom the country may honor for their noble leadership. Be stewards of all you possess.

If you and I trifle with our stewardship, we forfeit it. You say, how can we forfeit it? In various ways. We do it most of all by unfaithfulness. The man with the one talent was unfaithful and the Master took it away from him and gave it to the man who was faithful and who had accumulated ten talents. That which you have shall be taken away from you. How serious and how terrible is unfaithfulness! Where are the ancient nations who were unfaithful—ancient Babylon, Rome, Tyre, Sidon; where are they? Once proud and powerful, but recalcitrant and forgetful of God, they sleep in the cemetery of the doomed and defeated nations. God help America to be faithful!

The unfaithful organization, whatever it is, missionary, educational, or benevolent, if it loses sight of its great mission, is doomed. The unfaithful church—the bride of Christ—will have the candle-stick removed like the seven unfaithful churhes of Asia. The unfaithful family or individual man or woman who says, "This is mine," is wrong and there will be a prophet at the gate saying: "The day of accounting is come; the day of reckoning is here; give an account of your stewardship."

How can we forfeit our stewardship? We can do so by changed circumstances. Just the other day I was talking with a preacher who said, "I may not be able to preach anymore. (He was speaking in a whisper.) Oh, God forgive me if I was unfaithful when I did have a voice." Circumstances may change; your voice, your eyes, your health, your property may all fail. You have them today, but you may not have them tomorrow and it will not matter much whether you have

137

them or not, if you have not been a good steward of these potential blessings.

There was a great soul in Beaumont, Texas, who in the day of his prosperity said, "I want to provide a beautiful building for Baylor University." He gave that building which still stands as a monument to his benevolence. Later, the wheel of fortune turned and he lost his property, all of it, until he was left utterly stranded; and men of the world got around him and said, "Aha, don't you wish you had that money back that you put into that school building?" He said, "Not at all. It is all that I have saved. If I had kept that money I would have lost it too. I am thankful that I gave that building when I did."

God does not require us all to do some great thing for him, but he does require that we be faithful stewards of what he gives us. Ultimately every one of us will have to render unto God an account of our stewardship. Will that be a time of utter humiliation for us, or will it be a time of deep rejoicing as we hear the Master say, "Well done, good and faithful servant; . . . enter thou into the joy of thy Lord"? There are others who say, "We cannot take that step, we are not ready to go that far; but we do wish today to take the great step of the public commitment of ourselves to Christ, who alone forgiveth and saveth sinners. We will receive him as our Saviour and yield our lives to his control this Lord's Day morning, the first of the New Year, that Christ may forgive and cleanse and save and guard and guide and use us from this day forward and forever, according to his holy will." Come, and before all the people let the great confession be made of your choice of the Lord Jesus Christ as your Saviour and Master today and forevermore.

CHAPTER XII

The Unashamed Believer

CHAPTER XII

The Unashamed Believer

Whosoever believeth on him shall not be put to shame.

—Rom. 10:11

Paul discloses the central note of all evangelical preaching in this clear text as given in the tenth chapter of Romans, "For the Scripture sayeth, Whosoever believeth on him shall not be put to shame." Whatever Paul's theme, he always linked it up with Christ. Listen again to his ringing words when he had made a great plea: "I determined to know nothing among you save Jesus Christ and him crucified." Listen again as he talked about men glorying in this fact: "God forbid that I should glory save in the cross of our Lord Jesus Christ." Listen to him again as he talked about themes that men could speak upon when they came to preach, and said of himself: "We preach not ourselves, but Christ Jesus as Lord, and ourselves as servants for Jesus' sake."

Paul realized and affirmed that there is only one adequate hope and help for humanity, and such hope and help are to be found in Christ and in him alone. Surely it is the part of wisdom that we follow Paul in this great matter of giving our witness for Christ. He pointed people to Jesus as the only adequate hope and help for them for the present and for the unfolding and never-ending future.

Here then is the mission, the business of every friend and follower of Christ: to walk in the steps of this man Paul and give our witness, ever so clearly and so urgently, that men and women hearing our witness shall understand that there is just one way of salvation, and that way is Christ. This mat-

ter of witnessing for Christ and winning for Christ, of re-
minding everyone that salvation alone is by Christ, is a matter of vital and supreme moment for us all. The supreme
duty for all Christians in Dallas and in America and in the
world is to proclaim to all that there is one adequate hope
and help for mankind, just one, and that one is Christ.

The winning of souls to the side and service of Christ is the
primary and central and supreme and unceasing task of every
Christian in the world. You ask at once, "Of every Christian?"
And I reply without hesitation, "Yes, that is the supreme mission of every Christian." The early Christians believed that
so firmly that they went everywhere bearing their witness, and
within one generation they had made disciples throughout
the Roman Empire in such large numbers that the empire
of the Caesars had to take notice of Christianity. Those early
Christians believed that the first note in the marching orders
Jesus gave them, "Go ye therefore and make disciples of all
nations," should be taken literally.

When Christ came, Roman law had failed, Greek philosophy had failed, Oriental mysticism had failed; all had failed
when he came. He was the only remedy then; and there is
only one surviving remedy for mankind now. All have failed
now except one, and that one is Christ. The world has tried
big business, diplomacy, state-craft, war, secular education,
science, imperialism, communism, and they all have failed
to meet the needs of the human heart.

We are to remember that witnessing for Christ should be
the master passion of every Christian in the world, and especially of every preacher. Woe betide the people if the
preacher be not a true shepherd of souls. Of him it was said,
"I have made thee a watchman. If thou faileth to watch, and
evil shall overtake the one over whom I have appointed thee
to watch, then will I require his blood at thy hand." Oh, the
responsibilities of a preacher! I can well understand how
Rutherford, that glorious village preacher in Scotland gen-

erations ago, made his cry to God to help him help the people. In his diary he wrote:

> *Oh, if these souls of Anwoth*
> *Will meet me at God's right hand,*
> *My heaven will be two heavens*
> *In Emmanuel's land.*

The preacher is to care. Who else is to care? Parents are to care. They cannot abdicate or delegate their responsibilities. I do not see how any man can keep from having a shadow across his heart, darker and heavier than my words can say, when his family is going to ruin spiritually. One wonders how parents can go on with a child or children headed in the downward way. How can parents be worldly when their children are on the broad road that leadeth to destruction? Every time the Lord lays a baby on the hearts of young parents there goes with that child a commission, "Take this child and rear it for me." That commission is from God, and if parents put other things first and evil overtakes that child, one day with broken hearts those parents will stand in the gate as did David of old and wail out their poignant cry, "Oh Absalom, my son, Absalom, would God I had died for thee. Oh, Absalom, my son, my son!"

I have heard that cry in Dallas. How can parents be careless, be prayerless, be worldly, be indifferent, be inconsistent with the child or children being moulded and shaped by them for all time and eternity? How can a parent be careless when his child is un-anchored to Christ? The home is God's first institution for mankind. I repeat what I have said often in your hearing; I am more concerned about the American home than I am concerned about any other thing in America, and there is much in America that makes me anxious now. I am more concerned about America now than I have ever been before. I see drifts, signs, and influences that contain peril for our country. But I am more concerned about

143

the American home than I am concerned about any other one thing, for there seems to be a conspiracy to destroy the old-fashioned, quiet, prayerful, God-honoring home. In so many cases the American home has ceased to be the center of the family's interest. The primary business of parents is to train up their children in the nurture and admonition of the Lord. If they fail in that high and holy duty, what cause have they for satisfaction in their material wealth, their social standing, or their creature comforts? Their smiles are due to turn into tears, and what they thought were wings for high-flying will prove to be millstones about their necks to drown them in seas of sorrow, if their children are on the road to destruction, giving no evidence of interest in the supreme things of God and the human soul. Parents are to care for the spiritual welfare of their children.

Who else is to care? Teachers are to care. The teacher sits on a throne. He may have only six young boys, but he is on a throne. The teacher who does not understand that his opportunities and responsibilities for his pupils are enough to make God's archangels tremble should forsake the teacher's calling and not trifle with the high things of human life. Teachers are to care.

Sir Langston, a scholar and philosopher of the Reformation, rightfully said this: "To train one youth is a greater achievement than a military conquest." Teachers are to care, and in particular, Sunday School teachers. The Sunday School teacher who does not have a burden for the class and every member of it which will cause him to say, "My heart's desire and prayer to God is that every member of my class may be saved," should do one of two things. He should give up the class; or he should repent and do his best to bring each member of that class to a saving knowledge of Christ. Teachers are to care.

Everyone is to care. All Christians are to care. The humblest Christian under the sound of my voice can point souls to Christ. Every Christian has as much as one talent. Most of us have just one. Every Christian can point people to Christ. The needle-woman can, the washer-woman can, the humble clerk can, the grocery-man can, the cab-man can, the lawyer, the doctor, the banker, the teacher—every Christian can point people to Christ. That is our business, primary, central, supreme, and unceasing.

The truth that Paul stated in our text and that I am seeking to emphasize in this sermon is well illustrated in the stories concerning two men, one a Southern banker, and the other a Northern minister.

The man of the South was president of a large city bank that had three hundred employees. He became so deeply concerned about the spiritual condition of those employees that he called them all together for an evening meal, and they all came, with considerable anxiety as to why he had called them. After the dinner he arose and said, "I have called you together because I want, in the first place, to tell you how I appreciate you and your loyalty to this bank; and then I want to ask you to forgive me, if you can, for I have been a Christian for many years and yet I have never talked to any of you about the welfare of your souls. A Christian ought to do better than that. You, perhaps, have gained the impression that I think bank deposits are more important than the souls of people. I do not think that, but I have acted as though I did. I want you to forgive me if you can."

Then that bank president poured out his heart to that group in witness concerning the Saviour. The majority of them were already professed Christians as through tears and with uplifted hands they so indicated. The rest of them said they were not Christians. Then that banker turned preacher and exhorter with such earnestness that, ere a week had passed, he had won them all to Christ. What a blessed experience for that banker, those employees and that southern city!

The second man was the minister of a large Presbyterian Church in a Northern city. Months had gone by and not a soul had been converted. The pastor was greatly discouraged, so much so that he decided to ask the elders of the church to meet with him for a serious conference. When they came he said to them, "I am greatly discouraged. I am thinking that I should resign as your minister. People are not being converted and the main business of a church is to win the lost to Christ. I am wondering if I should resign."

Then the elders said, "Oh, no, Doctor, your preaching is very edifying."

The minister said, "Edifying for what? You elders, church leaders, come on Sunday morning and heaven alone knows where you are Sunday night. One in a dozen of you come to prayer-meeting, but where are the other eleven? Our church is failing in its God-given mission. The main reason for its existence is to save souls. Things will have to change or I will have to resign. Perhaps this church needs another minister and also another group of elders."

Then the minister asked the senior elder, "Did you ever win a soul to Christ in your life?" and the reply was, "Never." The same question was asked of every elder present and not one of them could say, "Yes, I have won somebody to Christ."

The tragedy of it all struck home to the hearts and consciences of those men. They were like Peter, James and John who slept while their leader sweat blood in the garden.

To make a long story short, those elders went forth on their main business that week, with the result that the next Sunday that church saw thirty men come to the altar and say, "We have found the Saviour and these elders led us to him." Oh, the joy that filled that preacher, those elders, that whole church and the angels in heaven! And we may be sure that the hearts of those thirty men and their families were also filled with gladness.

Oh, if my great board of deacons would respond as did those elders in that church of the North, I think my cup of joy would overflow. I think I would be ready to say with Simeon of old, "Now Lord, let thy servant depart in peace; for mine eyes have seen thy salvation."

Conl

Our text says, "Whosoever believeth on him (that is on Christ) shall not be put to shame." Certainly no believer can ever be ashamed of Jesus, for Jesus meets all the tests that may be applied. He never disappoints. He was perfect in his divinity and in his humanity. He never humiliates the true believer. But many believers are put to shame by their failure to do their Master's bidding. He said that his followers were to be his witnesses, that they were to seek the lost even as he came to seek and to save the lost, that as the Father sent him on the mission of salvation even so was he sending forth upon the same mission those who believed on him. Oh, the tragedy and the shame of it, that so many of those whom he has saved never put forth even one effort to seek out and win the lost to Christ by their own personal witness concerning their Saviour and Lord! It is enough to make angels weep, and it should fill the hearts of the disobedient and unfaithful followers with unspeakable shame. Multitudes of professed Christians and church members should be upon their knees begging God's mercy upon them for their sins of omission in the all-important matter of witnessing for Christ and seeking to lead the lost to him.

For some of you in this audience the day is far spent and you have no sheaf of souls you can lay at the feet of the Saviour when you come before his throne on that Great Day. You hope to receive a crown but it will be a starless crown unless you win some soul to Christ. While the day of opportunity is still yours put forth the effort, for the night cometh when no man can work. Resolve now in your deepest heart, that with God's help you will turn over a new leaf and pray that with his help you may be able to write on that new page the names of some whom you have led to the Lord.

Then, dear believer, you will not be put to shame. He that winneth souls is wise and experiences the deepest joy known to this world.

CHAPTER XIII

Bought with a Price

C H A P T E R   X I I I

Bought   with   a   Price

~~~~~~

Ye are not your own.

—I COR. 6:19

I N THE sixth chapter of Paul's first letter to the
Corinthians he gives us, in the closing sentences of that chapter, the text for our meditation together this morning. "And
ye are not your own, for ye are bought with a price; therefore
glorify God in your body, and in your spirit, which are God's."
When you read the context, and the context ought always to
be read in connection with any statement in the Scriptures, in
order to understand what the author is talking about, you
will see that Paul was dealing here with the sins of the body.
God attaches great importance to the human body. It is not
only a temple for the human spirit to dwell in, but it is also, to
a remarkable degree, a temple in which dwelleth the Spirit of
God.

The Bible distinctly tells us that the Spirit of the living
God dwelleth within us. Surely, then, the body ought not
to be profaned by unchastity, by uncleanness, by gluttony, or
by drink. The body is a creation to which God attaches great
honor and should not be polluted nor desecrated nor pro-
fanely defiled. Paul is here discussing that very subject. What
a delicacy of words he uses! What loftiness of motives he discloses! What faithfulness he exhibits through it all! And
out of it all he leads up to this great text: "Ye are not your
own, for ye are bought with a price; therefore glorify God in
your body and in your spirit which are God's." Great
thoughts emerge from this great statement. May the Holy
Spirit enable us to grasp the full meaning of it.

151

First of all, we see here the wonderful fact stated: "Ye are not your own," because you did not make yourselves. God made you. We are the creatures of his divine creation. A great argument is that. We are creatures and God is the Creator. He has indisputable rights in his creation. Paul could have pleaded that, but he did not.

Paul could have pleaded Providence. There is a watchful providence over us all. God's eye is on the sparrow. He paints every flower. He guides the wings of every bird. The dissolving clouds, the rolling oceans, the towering mountains, these are under the watchful care of God. He does not allow even a sparrow to fall to the ground, except by his permission. He himself tells us, "Ye are of much more value than many sparrows." Paul could have pleaded that, but he named neither creation nor providence as the great, main motive why we should live at our highest and best.

Paul pleaded Redemption. "Ye are bought with a price," even the precious blood of Christ. Not with gold and silver. much as the world treasures these metals. "Ye are bought with a price" even "the precious blood of Christ." History is filled with examples of slaves who have been redeemed with gifts, bought with silver and gold, and then set free. Here we are broken and beaten with moral lapse, loss and defeat and failure. But Jesus came and bought us from the bondage of Satan and sin. Jesus came and redeemed us. Here, then, is the highest fact pertaining to our life in this world. We have been bought with the "precious blood of Christ."

There is the fact of our birth. What a significant fact! We are born human beings, not reptiles in the forest, not beasts of the fields; we are created human beings. What a great fact is the creation of a human being, made in the image of God We all have been created in the image of God, and though desecrated and dragged down by sin, still as human beings we retain something of that marvelous creation in which God has divinely fashioned us.

However, if we fail to be redeemed from the bondage of sin, Christ tells us, "It would have been better for you if you had never been born." If we are to be enthralled by sin all our days, to be the servants of sin, to be led captive by Satan in his evil ways, to be the desperate victims of our sins. Christ himself reminds us it is better that we had never been born.

There is youth with its habit-forming period, with its decision period, with its inspiring, glowing period. What events these are all along in life! There comes a time when one fares forth to school and later along, may be, to college or university far away—important events! Then there comes the time when the graduation hour is reached—joyful felicitations from loved ones and friends are received. Happy hour! Then there comes the wedding day with all its sentiment and beauty and glory. Thus the days of life are unfolded with their battles and burdens and epochs and decisions. How important they all seem at the time!

But the most important fact in the universe of God which concerns our lives is the fact that Christ Jesus died for us. That fact claims priority over all other facts and influences in life. "Ye are bought with a price," even "the precious blood of Christ" who has been as a Lamb slain for sinners from the foundation of the world. That is the supreme fact to influence us throughout our lives.

We will not recall, I think, when we get home to the better land to live forever with our Lord, the fact that we had a little property or that we did not have it; that we were rich or that we were poor; that we gained a little prestige or did not; that we lived strongly and well in body or that we were weakened by ill health. We will recall instead the fact that the Son of God left his Father's house and came to earth for us, and confronted the law of God which said, "The soul that sinneth, it shall die." We will remember the fact that our vicariously suffering Saviour, our atoning Redeemer, our

Mediator, took the sinner's place and said, "I will suffer in his stead." The fact uppermost in the hearts of the redeemed in Heaven, I must believe, will be this fact in which we will glory with joy untold forever, that Christ redeemed us with his own precious blood on the cross. The song of the Christian should ever be:

> Redeeming love hath been my theme,
> And shall be 'till I die.

No wonder we sing so often now:

> There is a fountain filled with blood,
> Drawn from Emmanuel's veins,
> And sinners plunged beneath that flood,
> Lose all their guilty stains.

> The dying thief rejoiced to see,
> That fountain in his day.
> And there may I, 'though vile as he,
> Wash all my sins away.

> Dear dying Lamb, thy precious blood,
> Shall never lose its power,
> 'Till all the ransomed church of God,
> Be saved to sin no more.

> Then in a nobler, sweeter song,
> I'll sing thy pow'r to save,
> When this poor lisping, stammering tongue,
> Lies silent in the grave.

We will sing forever in the House of Life about redeeming love. Here is our central note, here is our gospel note, and the preacher who leaves this note out of his gospel does not have a gospel. The world is bludgeoned and beaten and defeated by sin, and men must have an atoning sin-bearer, a vicariously redeeming Saviour, or the world is doomed, defeated and destroyed.

Now, it follows inevitably, "Therefore glorify God in your body and in your spirit, which are God's." There is the inevitable consequence and Paul states both the negative and the positive aspects of it. "Ye are not your own, ye are bought with a price." Negatively, "ye are not your own"; positively, "ye are bought with a price." You belong to Christ body and spirit. Ye are not your own"; you belong to another and that other is Christ. You belong to him and that means you are not to profane that which is another's. Paul is pleading: "Do not desecrate young manhood or young womanhood; do not pollute and defile by unchastity and uncleanliness; do not mis-use your lives." You are not your own; you are bought by Christ, redeemed by him. Do not mis-use his property; do not profane your body.

The man with the one talent went and hid it and came back and reported to his master, "I was afraid and hid your talent." He was mis-using that which was not his own at all. He was playing with it, trifling with it. We are not to mis-use or abuse our gifts and resources. "Ye are not your own." The honest man does not want to encroach upon that which is another's. The man who would seek to mis-use his neighbor's property is neither good nor honest.

To whom do you belong and for what are you giving your life? Just here is the world-wide difference between men. Think of the difference between that clever infidel, Robert Ingersoll and that plain man, Dwight L. Moody.

Ingersoll was brilliant and gifted, we are told, but a scoffing infidel. Think of him laughing to scorn the Bible and the mighty things bound up with it. The teachings of the Bible concerning man's lost condition and man's eternal blessedness through Christ who died on the cross to redeem him from sin were to him just tales for old women and children. Think of his mockery and derisive laughter at it all!

Then, think of Moody, the plain, blunt business man, leaving his shoe store, going up and down the land with a Bible

155

in his hand, talking out of it so that two great continents were moved a little closer to God and heaven because of him. Moody recognized the absolute ownership of himself by Christ.

Everyone of us belongs either to Christ or Satan. Everyone of us is serving Christ or Satan. "No man can serve two masters: For either he will hate the one, and love the other; or else he will hold to one, and despise the other."

Cecil Rhodes was one of the great builders of his generation. He was the youngest son of an English clergyman, and his father gave him such education as he could with the limitations upon him as a preacher with a modest salary. This son was a good student and said that early in life these thoughts possessed him: "What is there in the world that can call out my best? Can money do it? No. Can prestige or fame do it? No. Can worldly pleasures do it? No. What can call out my utmost endeavor? Why," he said, "I will go down and dedicate my life to South Africa; poor, belated, and bedraggled and overborne by ignorance and superstition and every kind of down dragging perversity of life. I will go down there and give my life. I will make every dollar I can and put it into the redemption of South Africa." And that is what he did. His business adventures were all crowned with great success, and he poured his profits right back into the uplift and disenthrallment of South Africa, thus making it one of the valued lands of the British Empire.

And another was Daniel Ford, for a long time owner and publisher of *The Youth's Companion*. He was a modest man and a child of poverty. He went to a little Sunday School as a boy and was converted early in life. He became a Sunday School teacher, and later a Sunday School superintendent. He linked his life with great causes, and then labored in their behalf. He expressed the motivating purpose of his life in these words: "I belong to Christ, for he bought me, and therefore, he needs me here to voice my trusteeship for him to the utmost of my power." Out of that great, high principle come the great movements of the world. Out of that principle came the great missionary movement to win the world for Christ. Out of that principle comes the great temperance movement that we should have clean lives and not lead debauched, defiled, polluted lives. Out of that great principle comes the great movement of human sympathy for the poor and the needy and our effort to uplift and undergird and fortify the unfortunate in every way possible.

Daniel Ford of *The Youth's Companion* said, "I belong to Christ and I must make every stroke count for him." He had an extensive fortune when he died, and what did he do with it? He gave one hundred and fifty thousand dollars for the upkeep of his one unmarried child. He then went to his pastor and said, "Here are two and one half million dollars for the church and the causes fostered by the church."

Daniel Ford had the most exalted view of the church, and a man misses it utterly who does not have that view. The one supreme institution in the world in which all good things lie is the church of the living God. These general movements, missionary, educational and benevolent, would drag, and in one or two generations would die, but for the inspiring power of the church of the living God. Jesus knew what he was about when he fashioned the one institution, the church, and said, "The gates of hell shall not prevail against it."

Jesus was not mistaken when he fashioned his church and urged his followers to give to it their powers, their prayers and their loyal support, that its emancipating, life-witnessing power might reach to the ends of the earth.

To whom do you belong? To what? What is your motive in life? What are you living for? You are left here a few brief fleeting years to live for Christ, because you belong to him. Now he says, "Ye are not your own, ye are brought with a price," therefore glorify God in your body, in your spirit, in everything you have and are and can be, glorify God to whom you belong. Here is the meaning of life. Here is the high mission of life.

The selfish man is doomed, no matter who he is. He may be as brilliant as Napoleon, but he will have Napoleon's ill-fated doom. He may have success for a season, but it will turn into derisive mockery by and by. Selfishness is attended forever with defeat, doom and death.

We are to live for the Lord, and when Christian men and women are putting their best thought and loyalty and life and time and talents, their *all* into the one institution which Christ has fashioned, they are making their lives count, and count until time shall be no more and on throughout endless eternity.

What are you living for? Who is your Lord and Master? Are you living for Christ? Are you consulting his will? Are you asking, "Lord, what wilt thou have me to do? How can I make my life count for the highest and the best?" That is the mission and meaning of life. To whom do you belong? Who is your master? Who dominates your life? Oh, I remind you, if we live outside the will of God, we miss the meaning of life. We are left here a little while, not long for any of us. Therefore glorify God in your body, in your spirit, with your time, with your loyalty, with your love, with your talents, with all the gifts that make up your total trusteeship.

Now, since we are not our own, but belong to our Saviour who redeemed us, let us trust our all to him and go on utterly unafraid. Wars and rumors of war may bedarken the world. Christ lives and loves and reigns. "Because I live, ye shall live also." "My sheep hear my voice and I know them and they follow me, and I give unto them eternal life, and they shall never perish, neither shall any man pluck them out of my hand. My Father which gave them me, is greater than all, and no man is able to pluck them out of my Father's hand. I and my Father are one." Oh, since we belong to Christ, let us lean upon him trustfully that we may become

158

more than conquerors through him that loved us! Let us go on our way unafraid and undismayed.

> *Be not dismayed, whate'er betide,*
> *God will take care of you.*
> *Beneath His wings of love abide,*
> *God will take care of you.*
>
> *Through days of toil when heart doth fail,*
> *God will take care of you.*
> *When dangers fierce your path assail,*
> *God will take care of you.*
>
> *All you may need He will provide,*
> *God will take care of you.*
> *Nothing you ask will be denied,*
> *God will take care of you.*
>
> *No matter what may be the test,*
> *God will take care of you.*
> *Lean, weary one, upon His breast,*
> *God will take care of you.*

We are not left here through chance or accident. "My times are in thy hand, O Lord." "I will both lay me down in peace and sleep, for thou, Lord, only makest me to dwell in safety." "I will not be afraid of evil tidings, my heart is fixed, trusting in the Lord."

Now, since we belong to him, let us have joy in our bondage to him. If someone here says, "I do not belong to him," then I say to that one, surely you wish to come away from the side of Satan to the side of this Saviour who died for you by the shedding of his precious blood on Calvary's cruel cross as the price of your redemption. Here and now I beseech you to foreswear all allegiance to Satan and to sin and to the selfish

159

course in life, and to dedicate yourself utterly to Christ, the one and only rightful Lord and Master.

Wendell Phillips, one of the great reformers of this country, said that at the age of twelve years he heard Lyman Beecher speak, and the great man looked down at him and pointed his finger at him and said, "Son, you belong to Christ! Live for him!" And Wendell Phillips said that from that hour he was dedicated to give his all to Christ.

You remember, he lived the life of a stormy petrel. He was boycotted in his business whichever way he turned. He was hooted and hissed whenever he appeared on the streets of Boston. Rotten eggs pelted him and all kinds of insults were heaped upon him. He would go home at night to his invalid wife, and when she would see him come in and behold his weariness and his readiness almost to faint and to quit, she would say, "Wendell, you belong to Christ. Do not shilly-shally. Go back to your work and let them do to you as they please. You are working for humanity. You are working for Christ. Go bravely on."

Oh, that is a word for us all. Do not shilly-shally. You belong to Christ. Never follow Christ afar off, nor evade the issue when righteousness is involved. You belong to Christ. Represent him; incarnate his Spirit; live grandly the life he wants his friends to live. Be true as the needle to the pole, when you think of your allegiance to Christ and your trusteeship from him and for him.

Oh, young men and women, seek to be Christians after the mind and will of Christ! And you older men and women, all tangled in the affairs of time and earth walking in paths that lead to defeat, I plead with you to forsake those paths and turn unto Christ who died to save you and proffers his guidance and mercy and help. Accept him as your Saviour and Lord, here and now, and forever.

I beseech you to confess allegiance to Christ Jesus. I beseech you to accept the forgiveness, the mercy, the grace and the power which he offers you so freely. I implore you not to postpone this most important decision of all to what Satan suggests will be a more convenient season. In all probability there will be no more convenient time to accept and confess Christ as your Saviour and Lord and Master than this very hour. Jesus said, "Come unto me, and I will give you rest. Him that cometh unto me, I will in no wise cast out." Will you come now? God help you to decide aright even now!

CHAPTER XIV

The Supreme Gift to Jesus

CHAPTER XIV

The Supreme Gift to Jesus

But first they gave their own selves to the Lord.

—II Cor. 8:5

As we come to this first Lord's Day of the New Year, the one sentence that has kept ringing in my heart as a suitable word for us today is the oft quoted saying of Paul concerning the Macedonian Christians, "But first they gave their own selves to the Lord."

Paul is here praising the early Macedonian Christians in words remarkably gracious and heartening, as you observed while you listened to the Scriptural reading, a moment ago, from the eighth chapter of Second Corinthians. Praise from Paul was certainly noteworthy. He was no fulsome flatterer. He spoke words straight and direct and true. When men needed rebuking, Paul was just the man to give such rebuke. And now, when he finds an unusual case of devotion to Christ, and of sacrifice for Christ, and of glorious witnessing to the power of the grace of Christ, Paul sets it forth in this chapter in words that fairly breathe with beauty and blessing.

These early Macedonian Christians were sorely afflicted themselves, with their means of living pitifully reduced; yet out of their affliction and poverty they got together an offering for some needy people far away. Though themselves in dire distress, yet with all the good will of the givers and with a prayer for God's favor upon their united gifts they sent their offerings, voluntarily and joyfully, to far-away people who were in need. Paul makes a telling discourse upon such an unusual deed, and pays his tribute to it in a way that makes life loom larger and the possibilities of human nature seem grander as we read his tribute.

But the point of his praise is what we need to see clearly today; and that is that no man can please Christ and do his will as he wishes until the supreme thing is done toward Christ and for him, namely, until life itself is unreservedly laid on the altar for him. When one's life is fully laid on the altar for Christ, all else in service for him is easy and natural and blessed, because the greater includes the less. Just as long as a Christian proposes to serve God with little driblets of money and time and service, the Christian life is vitiated and stunted and misrepresented. But when a Christian faithfully apprehends the truth that the Christian life calls for the actual giving of life unto him who gave his life for us, then a thousand smaller questions are settled in one moment, and settled once for all.

There are two simple but practically vital truths that may be seen in this story of the Macedonian Christians whose conduct called forth such positive praise from Paul.

First, of all, these early Christians put the cause of Christ as the first thing in their lives. That was altogether praiseworthy and consistent and necessary. Where should Christ's cause be put? I am speaking this morning to an army of Chrsitian men and women, and upon you, one by one, I would press this question upon your deepest conscience. Where should Christ's cause be put by the friends of Christ? These early Christians clearly put it first in their lives. Untold mischief comes to Christian men and women, and to the vital cause they represent, when they haggle and fail to put Christ's cause first in their lives, to make it the center and heart of their thought and activity.

The most superficial views are often taken by Christians concerning the Christian life. It is sometimes vainly thought that if we can add largely to our numbers, then are we indeed making progress. It does not necessarily follow that an army

166

is making progress because it keeps adding soldiers to the ranks. The Bible never one time gives any such hint that an increase in numbers is the way of progress in the Christian warfare. The Bible never once gives any encouragement to the doctrine that we shall be strong according to our numbers. Indeed, we are warned again and again, by warnings direct and implied, as to the snare that there may be in numbers.

illus.

There stands out like some dark cloud the old story of David's numbering the kingdoms of Israel and Judah, to warn God's people forever that they must not put their confidence in numbers. Never once does God put the emphasis on numbers. Read the story of Gideon's vast army reduced to three hundred men, and see how God utterly discounts numbers. *GIDEON* Often it is given to us to see how God signalizes the mighty victories that may be obtained by a small group consecrated and definitely committed to his program. It is not "How many do we count in the kingdom of God?" but "How much do we weigh?" It is not quantity in the kingdom of God that counts but it is quality. You can sometimes put your hand on one man in a community who seems to have the power of a thousand ordinary Christian men. His very nod is empire; his very footfall is law; the very crook of his finger is power. The explanation is that he lives his religion. It is not duration that counts in human life, but intensity. Some men die at thirty and have done more for humanity than others dying at one hundred and thirty. The first mentioned live while they live with the one motive of doing the will of God.

B.) Again, it is manifest that men sometimes have the mistaken conception if they had more money they could forward Christ's cause in a victorious way. They were never more mistaken. Never one time is the emphasis in the Bible put upon material, visible resources. I have no sympathy at all with the anarchistic outcry that is sometimes heard against money. I do not hesitate to say that men who can make

167

money ought to make it—legitimately, to be sure—for all il-
legitimately gained money is a curse to him who gains it.
Men who have gifts in the world of business, commanding
gifts, strategic gifts, who can amass money legitimately and
properly, ought to do so; but money in the kingdom of God
is not the supreme thing at all. The early disciples of Jesus
were without money, and yet they shook the Roman empire
to its foundation with their spiritual power. They did not
have vast bank accounts, and yet the pagan empire was shot
through with gleams of heavenly light in one short generation. Money is not the supreme thing in the kingdom of God.
Full many a time it is a terrible handicap, a perilous
hindrance. Full many a time men turn to it instead of to the
arm invisible and almighty. To the degree that men put their
confidence in human, visible, material resources, to that degree are they weak and not strong at all.

What then is the supreme thing to be laid to heart in the
kingdom of God? It is pointed out here for us by these Macedonian Christians. It is to put Christ's cause as the first
thing in our thinking and doing, literally to put it first, and to
build around it as the center of all our thought and all our
activity. These early Christians, by the glorious example de-
scribed here for us by Paul, point the way for us, if we would
make the Christian life a thing of ever-growing happiness and
ever-increasing triumph over the world about us. How all
things would be changed about us if we would put first things
first!

Now, Christ's cause is to be put first by Christians—not off
in a corner, treated as some stepchild, unloved, and in the
way. Christ's cause is to be put first everywhere, and forever
to be put first. That is the need of the world today. The only
kingdom that shall last, the one kingdom that shall ultimately
break to pieces every other kingdom, the one kingdom whose
right it is to have undisputed sway in all the earth, is Christ's
kingdom; and Christ's friends should always and everywhere

put his kingdom first. That is the outstanding need of the world today. "Seek ye first the kingdom of God and his righteousness." Seek it first—not secondly, nor thirdly, nor subordinately, nor optionally, nor incidentally.

"Put my cause first" is ever the call of Jesus to his people. Put it first when you go to the bank. Put it first when you stand before court and jury. Put it first when you go from house to house ministering to the sick. Put it first when you stand in the high place of the teacher. Put it first in the pulpit. Put it first in the market-place. Put it first in the realm of government. "Put my kingdom, my cause, my will, first," is forever Christ's call. Christians are to hear this call, and act on it, and live it, and relate all life to it. That is the world's first need—to put Christ first.

Paul stated it for us when he said, "To me to live is Christ," or, freely translated, "To me to live is for Christ to live over again." Said Paul, "I am to think his thoughts, and to talk his talk, and to do his deeds as best I can, and to live his life, and to offer myself as did he for humanity." That is the business of a Christian in this world. What other business could a Christian have? After I am redeemed from the curse of law by Jesus, who died for me, the Just for the unjust, the Sinless for the sinner, I am left for a little while in the earth to reincarnate the spirit, the teaching, the life, of Jesus; and I am to put him first. So that when Paul said, "Ye are not your own; ye are bought with a price. Therefore, glorify God in your body and in your spirit, which are his," he was just stating the simplest, plainest, fairest truth that can be put into human words. You Christian men and women literally belong to Christ. I charge you therefore to put his cause where it ought to be. Let his will be regnant in all human life just as it ought to be. Then even this earthly life is, indeed, a thing of surpassing glory.

You will observe that these early Macedonian Christians, in all their various callings, thus enthroned Christ's will and made it regnant in all their daily temporal affairs. The religion of the Lord Jesus Christ is not simply a showy business for Sunday. If you are going to make any choice and put your best foot forward at some particular time in Christian living, do it yonder in the market-place, rather than here when you are singing some beautiful hymn. Do it in the home, where the nervous, impatient child is taxing you to the limit. Live for Christ out there where you closely touch humanity, where all the sharp currents of life clash. There put the will of Christ first.

These early Christians in all their daily avocations put Christ's cause first. Oh, that is what we need, what we supremely need. A man will fail miserably if he is a schemer and a cheat yonder in his business and a pious, long-faced saint here in church. If the teacher forgets and is a nervous scold in the schoolhouse where plastic life is being touched and shaped by her every minute, that teacher is a failure. What the world needs is for this leaven of Christianity to be incarnated in our lives as we touch humanity the six busy days in the week as well as on the Lord's Day. The grocery man ought to be better, and the laundry man, and the messenger boy, and the butcher, and the telegraph boy, and the doctor, and all the rest, because you and I cross their paths and look into their faces, and greet them for a moment in life's daily battle. Our Christianity is to be radiant out there in the midst of the seething humanity which is dying without God. It was so with these early Christians, because they put Christ's cause first.

What a glorious day that will be—may God speed its full triumph!—when in all callings and among all classes and conditions of humanity shall be realized that noble injunction of Paul: "Whether ye eat or drink, or whatsoever ye do, do all to the glory of God." I can see how the modest teacher, just as truly as any prophet in his pulpit, can glorify God at her far-reaching task. I can see how the lawyer, standing before court and jury, can mightily glorify God, as he pleads for the fundamental principles of righteousness and justice and mercy. I can see how the financier, and the struggling girl with her typewriter, and the needlewoman, the farmer, the man driving the dray—humanity in all its phases and at all its tasks out there in the big battle of life—can glorify God as really as did Paul, if each one will simply put Christ's cause where the Macedonian Christians put it—put it first.

And here in your own modest circles of life there are men in this task, and women in that, who are incarnating the ideals of Jesus, and are putting his cause first, and they are positively and constantly blessing humanity. God speed the day when Christians, when you and I here in this meeting-house this first Lord's Day morning of the New Year, shall understand that what Christ waits for and asks at our hands is that we will do in life what we are here to do! That we will have the right sense of our vocation! And that we will relate ourselves to the one embracing task that we are in the world for, here in the little vestibule of time preceding eternity, to put Christ's cause first, and then pass from time to be with him in the larger House of Life, where all the conditions of life are perfect forevermore!

There is another vital truth to be emphasized. The secret of such wonderful devotion on the part of these Macedonian Christians is explained in the very words of the brief text: "But first they gave their own selves to the Lord." The crux of the whole matter of living the Christian life is stated here in this sentence: "But first they gave their own selves to the Lord."

Note carefully the words: "But first they gave their own selves to the Lord." They gave themselves. It is just at that point that we most sadly fail as Christians. We propose to give Jesus little compartments in our lives, and then desire him to leave us to ourselves with the larger compartments. Oh, that is the tragedy of our Christianity! These early Chris-

171

tians just did what a Christian is in the world for, what you and I are here for—namely, to do Christ's will, to represent Christ, to be his witness, to be his friend, to carry forward his kingdom, to make victorious his will everywhere. If we can carry out his will by ill health better than by good health, let ill health come! If we can do it better by poverty than by riches, let us have poverty! If we can do it better to be persecuted and hunted and sent to our graves misunderstood, Lord, let it be that way! Thy will be enthroned and made victorious through us, come as it will, cost what it may! It is not a theory that you and I are inescapably responsible for the doing of the will of God; that is the pre-eminent fact of life.

I have told you before of scenes I have witnessed and lessons I have learned in connection with the camp-meetings I have attended with the cattlemen, here and there, in the great West. It is one of the most refreshing joys of my life thus to be with them. They are heroes and empire builders. One morning I preached to a great group of cattlemen, gathered in a cleft of the mountains, perhaps a thousand men, on this searching text: "Ye are bought with a price; therefore, glorify God in your body, and in your spirit, which are God's." And that morning I was making the insistence that Christ should be the absolute Master of life, just as I am making it this morning. When the service was done, one of those cattlemen locked his arm in mine and said, "If you are willing, we will go for a walk. I have something to say to you."

And up the long mountain canyon we took our walk, more than a mile away from the camp-grounds. He said not a word as we were going. It was evident that he had something serious to say, and I waited for him to break the silence. When we were more than a mile away, he turned and faced me and said, "I want you to pray a dedicatory prayer for me." I said, "What do you wish to dedicate?" And then he said with sobs,

172

"I never knew until today that I am responsible to Jesus for my property. I have not been a Christian long, and I have not heard much about him, and I do not know much about what he expects of me. I never knew until you preached to-day that all these thousands of cattle, every hoof of them, that I have said were mine are not really mine, but that they belong to Christ, and that I am simply his administrator, his trustee, his steward. Never until today did I know that. And I never knew until today that these twenty-five miles and more of spreading ranch lands that I have said were mine are not mine at all, but his; that the title to every acre is in him; not until today did I know that. Now," he said, "I want you to bow down here and tell him for me that I will take my place; I will accept my stewardship; I will be his administrator on his estate. And then when you are through, I wish to pray."

Of course I prayed the best I could, the man consenting and assenting, with sobs and words, as I prayed. And when I had finished I waited for him to pray. He waited some minutes before he could speak sobbing, like a little child; and when, at last, he did speak, he said, "Master, am I not in a position now to give you also the loved one for whom I have long been praying? Am I not in a position now to give him to you? Along with all else, I do give him to you; save him for your glory; I give him to you today forever." We walked back to the camp, and not a word was said on the return journey. Then the day wore to evening, and the men again came together for worship, and I stood before them once more to preach. Nor had I preached a dozen minutes until a wild young fellow on the outskirts of the great crowd of a thousand cowmen rose up and said, "I cannot wait until that man is done his sermon to tell you that I have found the Lord!"

Do you doubt that there was a vital and fundamental connection between the right relation of that ranchman to Jesus Christ and the homecoming of him for whom he prayed? Oh, there is no telling, my brothers, how much power a man

173

may have to drive back Satan and beat down the very mountains of sin; there is no telling how much helpful power any man or woman may have, would have, even you and I, if only we will relate ourselves to the will of Christ like we ought. These early Christians did that, and the glory of God was over them beyond all words to tell.

You will notice that they did it voluntarily. Paul said, "They were willing of themselves." Nobody coerced them. Nobody drove them. Nobody scolded them. Nobody sought to wheedle money out of them by questionable pleas. God pity us! I have no respect for that kind of thing in religion. Here these men came, and they laid themselves, their very lives, on the altar for Christ. When a man does that supreme thing for Christ, is there any problem in his giving? Is there any problem in his giving money or time or talk or service? When the supreme thing has been given to Christ, you have gone to the heart of the Christian life, and then the Christian life can be made a great sun, lighting up the darkness near and far, and piloting many in the ways of righteousness.

Here is the test and here is the measure of our power to bless humanity. I tell you, no matter how brilliant a man is, no matter how gifted, no matter how generous, if he will not put his life into the service of Christ, he shall come short of the supreme thing. Life must be given for life. Life must make its impact on life. Far more than all the checks you can ever write is the writing of yourself into the right kind of service for a weary, sinful humanity. Incomparably better than any check that you will ever lay on the altar of Christ is for you to lay yourself on Christ's altar. You may have bewailed the fact that you lived from hand to mouth and could not put your dollars on the altar for Jesus as do others; but you could put something on the altar for Christ in comparison with which money seems but as a trifle. "I seek not yours, but you." That means that Christ seeks your manhood, your womanhood, your peronality, your individuality, your reputation, your character, your tongue, your brain, your example,

174

your very life. Humanity waits for that, and the kingdom of God comes—comes with power, comes to conquer, when Christian men and women put themselves, their lives, on the altar for their King and Redeemer.

That is the lesson for us today. That is the supreme lesson out of this old story. O preachers, you and I shall make pitiful progress in our exalted calling if we do not die to self and live to Christ! O Sunday-school worker, you will make slow progress if you have imagined you have discharged your Christian task when you have sat before your class once a week, for forty-five minutes or less, and have said a few things about the lesson. There are no secularities in the right kind of a Christian life. You and I are to put ourselves on Christ's altar twenty-four hours a day, living for Christ, serving or resting or eating or suffering, all for Christ. That is the supreme lesson we are to learn and to translate into daily deed.

Have you thus given yourself to Christ? O my friends, what is your spiritual condition today? Are you halting Christians, derelict Christians, duty-neglecting Christians, backslidden Christians, with your years hurrying like the flying clouds? Are you to go on like that until, some evening when the shadows of the night come to shroud the world, you come down to sudden death and startle your family with the gasp, "I have lived with practically no thought of Christ at all"? O men and women, the one thing that makes life really great is that we are here for a little season to do the Father's will, just like Jesus who came down from heaven, saying, "My meat is to do the will of him that sent me, and to finish his work." Is that your thought of life, your effort in life? Are you related to Christ today as you ought to be? We ought willingly to go through fire and flood to do anything Christ wishes at our hands, when we remember what He did and does for us. He gave his all for me. Yon cross was for me. That bloody sweat in Gethsemane was for me. That cry after cry, while the world was darkened, and the earth was shaking and the sun would not shine on that shameful scene, all that was for me.

175

O soul, is gratitude dead within thee? O man, hast thou lost all sense of the eternal properties? After what Christ did for us, surely we are ready to go any length for him.

Are there those here today who say, "Sir, we never did begin the Christian life at all"? Then, I ask, don't you think it is high time that you awake out of sleep? The day is far spent. Opportunity is passing, even now. Don't you think it is time today to be rightly related to Jesus? I wonder if there are not duty-neglecting Christians present who will say, "Without waiting to confer with flesh or blood, today I renew my vows with God, I do my duty today. Down in my deepest conscience I hear a voice, a clamant voice, a voice calling me to active service in Christ's church; I will obey today."

We are going to sing one of the great prayer-hymns as our hymn of invitation:

Take my life and let it be
Consecrated, Lord, to Thee.

As we sing this blessed song, surely there are those here who will come down the aisles of this Church accepting and confessing Christ as Saviour and Lord. And others will come to take their place among us by letter of transfer. And are there not others who will come declaring their purpose to give Christ first place in their lives as they have never done before? Come and God bless you as you come!

176